Masterpieces of the
Louvre

6

An Encyclopaedic Museum
PREFACE BY HENRI LOYRETTE

8

Eight Centuries of History
BY JEAN-FRANÇOIS LASNIER

22

Near Eastern Antiquities
BY DOMINIQUE BLANC

48

Islamic Art
BY DOMINIQUE BLANC

54

Sculptures
BY JEAN-FRANÇOIS LASNIER

Contents

28

Egyptian Antiquities
BY JEAN-FRANÇOIS LASNIER

38

*Greek, Etruscan and
Roman Antiquities*
BY JEAN-FRANÇOIS LASNIER

64

Decorative Arts
BY JEAN-FRANÇOIS LASNIER

72

Paintings
BY MANUEL JOVER

112

*Visitor information
and plans*

An Encyclopaedic Museum

An hour, a day, a weekend… all our visitors are free to explore the Louvre at their own rhythm, as their desires dictate. Whether one chooses to see – or revisit – the classic masterpieces, or sets off in search of the more secret works that are revealed only to the curious, away from the crowds, visiting this museum and former palace of the Kings of France is first and foremost a pleasure.

With more than thirty-five thousand works on display in the departments of Near Eastern Antiquities, Egyptian Antiquities, Islamic Art, Greek, Etruscan and Roman Antiquities, Sculptures, Paintings and Decorative Arts, the Louvre is one of the biggest museums in the world. It is a real-life encyclopaedia that covers nearly ten thousand years of human creativity, from 8,000 BCE to 1848, offering an incomparable panorama of arts and civilisations.

Rich with a history written over the years by the artists, curators, collectors, givers and patrons who have enriched its collections, the Louvre is no less an institution that is constantly on the move. Temporary exhibitions, new hangings and new acquisitions all reflect the constant concern to make the Louvre a living place, as do the regular invitations to contemporary artists to institute a dialogue with the architecture of the Louvre and works from past centuries.

More than ever, today's Grand Louvre is looking to the future, which it is building alongside the Louvre-Lens (to open in 2010) and the Louvre-Abu Dhabi (2013). As ever, its priorities are to facilitate access, develop information and mediation, and improve the comfort of the eight million or more visitors who come every year to delight in the treasures of the museum.

HENRI LOYRETTE
Director of the Louvre

Eight Centuries of History

From the top of the pyramid, eight centuries of history are watching us. For it was in 1190 that Philip Augustus decided to build a castle dominated by a keep thirty metres high. Under Charles V, the defensive role of this fortress was reduced by the construction of a new Parisian wall. The Louvre was now transformed into a true royal residence, a place of splendour (known to us only from paintings and miniatures). Henceforth, the Louvre was the palace where monarchic power was affirmed with the greatest ostentation.

Starting in the reign of Francis I, the last Valois, followed by the Bourbons, remodelled the palace by demolishing, rebuilding and enlarging. The construction of the Palais des Tuileries, between 1564 and 1572, prompted an irresistible westwards movement, symbolised by the Grande Galerie. The ambitious work undertaken by Louis XIV, the doubling of the Cour Carrée and the Colonnade, preceded a new change: in 1678, the Court moved to Versailles, leaving the palace to the Academies, including the Academy of Painting and Sculpture. The organisation of a Salon in 1699 can be considered the first art exhibition at the Louvre. Many academicians, such as Jean-Siméon Chardin, also benefited from quarters there. It was therefore perfectly logical for a decree of 1791 to dedicate the palace to the 'union of all the monuments of the arts and sciences'. The Revolutionary government thus met the wishes of many eighteenth-century art lovers who had argued for the creation of a museum at the Louvre. On 10 August 1793, the Muséum Central des Arts opened in the Salon Carré and the Grande Galerie. Constituted by royal collections and works seized during the Revolution, the holdings were soon swelled by booty brought back by the Revolutionary armies: Italy, Germany and the Netherlands paid their tribute to the victor, and a fantastic migration of works began, towards the new 'Musée Napoléon'. The fall of the Emperor and the restitution of these works sounded the knell of this universal museum. However, throughout the nineteenth century, and under successive governments, the Louvre worked to extend the cultural scope of its acquisitions: the Egyptian Department opened in 1827, the Assyrian Museum in 1847, then the Mexican, Algerian and ethnological museums in 1850. The Naval Museum also moved in to the Louvre under the reign of Charles X. Then came Napoleon III. In 1852, extension work on the Louvre was

launched, under the direction of Visconti, who was succeeded by Lefuel. The palace was linked to the Tuileries on the north side, and four internal courtyards were created on each side of the Cour Napoléon.

An administrative and cultural complex, the museum continued to grow and new museums were created in Paris to house the Asian collections and Impressionist paintings. In 1981, President Mitterrand decided that the museum would occupy the entire Louvre complex. The Ministry of Finance, then housed in the north wing, duly moved out and the collections of Northern European painting, decorative arts and Near Eastern antiquities moved in. The reconfiguration of the site was entrusted to Ieoh Ming Pei, who coordinated the team of architects. Inaugurated in 1989, the pyramid at the centre of the Cour Napoléon was the heart of his intervention, articulating all the different spaces in the museum, and housing all the public amenities and ticketing. However, the opening of the Richelieu wing in 1993 was not a culmination but the beginning of new transformations, the highlight of which is the creation of new galleries of Islamic Art, to open in 2010.   JEAN-FRANÇOIS LASNIER

Above:
THE SALLE SAINT-LOUIS
(The medieval Louvre)

Following double pages:
1st double page:
SALLE DES CARYATIDES
(Greek Antiquities)

SALLE DU MANÈGE
(Roman Antiquities)

DARU STAIRCASE
(Winged Victory of Samothrace)

2nd double page:
THE COUR MARLY
(Sculptures)

3rd double page:
THE SUMMER APARTMENTS
OF ANNE OF AUSTRIA
(Roman Antiquities)

GALERIE D'APOLLON
(Decorative Arts and
Crown Diamonds)

4th double page:
MONA LISA ROOM
(Italian Painting)

SALLE MOLLIEN
(French Romantic Painting)

5th double page:
GRANDE GALERIE
(Italian Painting)

6th double page:
GRAND SALON OF THE
NAPOLÉON III APARTMENTS

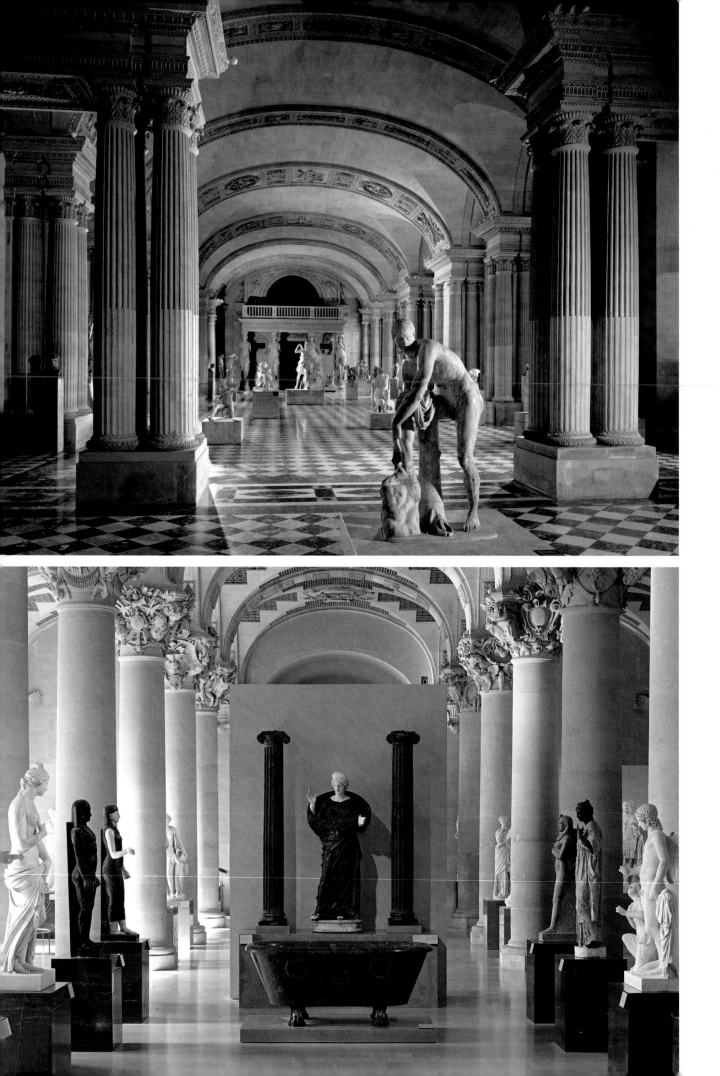

Near Eastern Antiquities

Just as much as the Egyptian Antiquities, the Near Eastern Antiquities hark back to the golden age of French archaeology in the Near and Middle East in the nineteenth and early twentieth centuries. The long-standing practice of sharing archaeological finds between the country of origin and foreign archaeologists helped establish French collections at the international forefront. As a result, the Louvre can boast some outstanding pieces that evoke the first known civilisation, the one that invented writing and law in Mesopotamia. Extending from the fourth millennium BCE to the birth of Islam in the seventh century CE, its collections cover a vast geographical area that takes in Mesopotamia, Iran, Central Asia, the Indus Valley, North Africa and the

Arabian Peninsula. The collections are organised chronologically and subdivided into geographical zones so as to highlight the phenomenon of rival city-states in Iran and Mesopo-

tamia. Excavations at Tello in 1877 initiated the discovery of Sumerian civilisation in the third millennium BCE, and led to the creation of the Department of Near Eastern Antiquities in 1881. Mari, the bastion of French archaeologists, proved to be the major centre of the Mid-Euphrates region. It was at Khorsabad (near today's Mosul) that in 1843 the French consul Paul-Emile Botta discovered the

vestiges of the palace of Sargon II, king of Assyria, now masterfully recreated in the museum. Susa, a city going back over six thousand years, was one of the capitals of Darius I, emperor of the Persians. The 'Frieze of Archers" that decorated the walls of his palace is one of the jewels of the collections. The Levant and Arabia (southern Syria and Yemen) began to show signs of cultural vitality in the fourth millennium, and this continued at a time when Greek influence was spreading well beyond the Mediterranean. There is eloquent evidence of all this at the Louvre, especially in the statuary.

DOMINIQUE BLANC

▲ PICTOGRAPHIC TABLET
*Late Uruk period (3100–2900 BCE),
Mesopotamia, Iraq. Limestone,
4.5 x 4.3 x 2.4 cm.*

This tablet bears some of the first
known 'written' signs, before
the invention of cuneiform script.
The end of the fourth millennium was
a golden age for Mesopotamian
civilisation, when it expressed itself
through art and architecture
glorifying the quasi-divine figure
of the king. A flourishing economy
proved conducive to the emergence
of these moving graphic marks
engraved in stone.

▶ EBIH-IL, THE SUPERINTENDENT
OF MARI
*Mari, Syria, circa 2400 BCE. Gypsum,
eyes inlaid with lapis lazuli, shell,
bitumen, H. 52.5 cm.*

This is the most sophisticated statue
from a set of male and female
likeness shown either standing or
seated, but most usually with their
hands together, all wearing the
kaunake, a long sheepskin skirt.
There being no direct link to the
iconography of power, it is hard to
place their function. This figure of the
Superintendent Ebih-il (his name is
engraved on his shoulder) was found
on the site of the temple of the
goddess Ishtar at Mari. It is not
known whether it is an ex-voto,
a votive statue or an offering.

▲ GUDEA, PRINCE OF LAGASH
Statue 'with the overflowing vase'
Tello, ancient Girsu, Iraq, circa 2120 BCE.
Dolerite, H. 62 cm.

Excavations at Tello unearthed large
numbers of black diorite representations
of the city's main rulers. A score of
these, dating from the 'Sumerian
Renaissance', represent Gudea, prince
of the independent kingdom of Lagash.
They differ markedly from the
traditional representations of rulers
with beard, chignon, turban and long
loincloth. Here, the fish-rich water
overflowing from the vase is an allegory
of the abundance and fertility embodied
by the king.

▶ VICTORY STELE OF NARAM-SIN
Akkadian Dynasty, reign of Naram-Sin
(2254–2218 BCE), discovered at Susa,
Iran; origin: Mesopotamia (Iraq). Pink
limestone, 200 x 105 cm.

This finely carved victory stele attests
the flourishing of Sumero-Akkadian
culture. As guarantor of the universal
order, the figure of the king crowns
a dynamic, stepped composition. Like
the sun god climbing the cosmic
mountain, Naram-Sin is represented
as the victorious leader of his armies,
trampling underfoot the dismembered
bodies of his vanquished enemies.

▲ **THE FRIEZE OF ARCHERS**
Susa, Iran, palace of Darius I, circa 510 BCE.
Polychrome glazed siliceous brick, 475 x 375 cm. Detail.

This decorative frieze, one of the emblems of the Near
Eastern Antiquities collections, evokes an army. But are
these archers in parade uniform, seen in profile with
quivers over their shoulder and their spears in their
hands, the guards of Darius I, or an ideal image of the
Persian people? The innumerable fragments forming this
frieze were found in the apadana (a freestanding
hypostyle hall). It is thought that these friezes may have
covered the exterior walls of the palace, extending over
hundreds of metres.

◄ **LAW CODE OF HAMMURABI**
First dynasty of Babylon, reign of Hammurabi
(1792–1750 BCE), discovered at Susa, Iran,
origin: Mesopotamia, Iraq. Basalt, 225 x 65 cm. Detail.

This stele is undoubtedly the most famous work from the
age of Hammurabi, the sixth king of the Amorite dynasty
who forged a union of the city-states of Mesopotamia
around his capital, Babylon. The 'code' is a collection
of laws and exemplary legal decisions, detailed in
a total of 3,500 lines engraved in basalt. At the top
of the stele, wearing a long robe and a wide-brimmed hat,
Hammurabi stands before Shamah, god of justice, who
can be identified by the symbols of his power, the circle
and rod, and the flames rising from his shoulders.

► **WINGED HUMAN-HEADED BULL**
Assyrian empire, reign of Sargon II (721–705 BCE),
Khorsabad, ancient Dur-Sharrukin, Iraq.
Gypseous alabaster, 420 x 436 cm.

The palace complex that Sargon II built on a ten-hectare
plot a few kilometres outside Nineveh (today's Mossul)
was designed to outshine all earlier palaces by its sheer
architectural scale and profuse ornamentation. Placed
at the main vaulted gates, these pilasters in the form
of winged, human-headed bulls were genies whose role
it was to ward off evil spirits. The presentation in the
Cour Khorsabad offers a reconstitution of this
spectacular architecture.

Egyptian Antiquities

The Department of Egyptian Antiquities can be seen as the finest flower of a French passion that grew in the sands of Egypt in 1798. Embodying the close connection between the Louvre and the banks of the Nile, the first director of the museum under the Consulate and Empire, Dominique-Vivant Denon, also accompanied Bonaparte on his Egyptian expedition and, on his return, published Voyage dans la Haute et Basse-Égypte, an account whose popularity contributed to the birth of French Egyptology. Following in his footsteps, a series of tutelary figures watched over the rise of the discipline in close liaison with the museum. The first

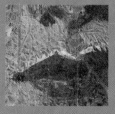

of these pioneers, Jean-François Champollion, was not only the man who deciphered the hieroglyphs, but also the founder of the Louvre's Egyptian Department in 1826. In this capacity he organised the acquisition of several major collections representing some 9,000 pieces. In 1852–53, Auguste Mariette, who had been sent on a mission by the Louvre, sent back some 6,000 new objects. In the

middle of the nineteenth century, Egyptology entered a new era, that of the sharing of excavations, which put an end to the pillaging of archaeological treasures. Thanks to this system set up by Mariette, now Director of Antiquities in Cairo, the Louvre's collections would benefit from constant enrichment, making it one of the leading museums in this field. Their extent has called for a complete redeployment, which was inaugurated in 1997. The new presentation makes it possible to follow the parallel developments of life in Ancient Egypt and Egyptian art, from the Neolithic era to the Coptic period.   JEAN-FRANÇOIS LASNIER

► **STELE OF THE SERPENT KING (DETAIL)**
1st dynasty, circa 3100 BCE. Provenance: Abydos.
Limestone, 143 x 65 x 25 cm.

Discovered by the archaeologist Emile
Amelineau in 1896, this stele in low relief stood
at the heart of the royal funerary monument
of Abydos in Upper Egypt. Surrounded by stelae
of courtiers, it marked the tomb of one of the
first pharaohs of the dynastic era.
The monumental hieroglyphs show that a
symbolic system relating to the royal person had
already been established in this early epoch.
Set inside his palace, surrounded by thick walls,
the sovereign's name is figured by the cobra,
that is, the hieroglyph reading *dj*. The serpent
king is placed under the protection of the falcon
god Horus, as all his successors would be.

▼ **SPHINX HEAD OF THE KING DJEDEFRE**
Old Kingdom, 4th dynasty, reign of Djedefre
(2565-2558 BCE). Provenance: Abu Roash.
Quartzite, originally painted, 26 x 33.5 cm.

The son of Cheops, Djedefre chose to have his
funerary monument built at Abu Roash, four
kilometres north of Giza. This fragment was
found in the upper temple beside his pyramid.
It may have been part of a sphinx with the
pharaoh's features. The traits are delineated
with great precision. Looking beyond the
conventions of Egyptian art, such as symmetry,
it is clear that the artist sculpted this life-sized
face with a real concern for individualisation
and anatomical truth.

► **GREAT SPHINX OF TANIS**
Old Kingdom, circa 2600 BCE, Tanis.
Granite, 183 x 480 x 154 cm, 9.5 tons.

This sphinx was so popular with rulers from
the 12th to the 22nd dynasties that several of
them had their names engraved on it. Although
a ruler from the Middle Kingdom did likewise,
it seems most likely that this sphinx was
sculpted under the 4th dynasty, like the famous
Giza sphinx, with which it shares a number
of characteristics, including its expression
of placid yet implacable power. The position
of the Giza monument, facing the sun, indicates
solar symbolism: by its twofold nature, as lion
and man, the sphinx manifests the union of the
king and Re, the sun god, from whom it derives
its protective power.

The Seated Scribe

Old Kingdom, 4th or 5th dynasty, circa 2600-2350 BCE, Saqqara.
Painted limestone, inlaid eyes in rock crystal, magnesite,
copper arsenic alloy, wood (nipples), 53.7 x 44 x 35 cm.

Discovered by Auguste Mariette in 1850, the *Seated Scribe* has become the emblem of the Department of Egyptian Antiquities, captivating visitors with its extraordinarily acute, life-like gaze. Behind this magical effect there is a technical feat: to make the Scribe's eyes the sculptor inserted into the ocular cavity a piece of white magnesite with red veins, in which is set a cone of rock crystal, glued with a touch of colour that simulates the iris. The delicacy of the details, set off by the remarkably well-preserved colour, heightens the naturalism of the figure. Likewise, his slight chubbiness, if conventional in representations of scribes, gives the figure a touching humanity. Far from being simple servants, scribes had such an aura that the princes of the Old Kingdom sometimes had themselves represented in that role. Sadly, the absence of inscriptions and the confused circumstances in which the figure was discovered mean that we cannot identify the person depicted.

▲ THE GODDESS HATHOR
WELCOMES SETHOS I
New Kingdom, 19th dynasty, 1303–1290 BCE.
Fragment from the wall of the tomb of
Sethos I, Valley of the Kings, Luxor.
Bas-relief. Painted limestone, 226 x 105 cm.

The founder of the 19th dynasty, Sethos I
was the father of Ramesses II.
Discovered by Champollion, this bas-
relief kept all its shimmering colours and
delicate decoration during the years
it was shut away in the secrecy of the
tomb. It represents the deceased ruler
meeting Hathor, goddess of the West,
which was the final abode of the dead.
The menat necklace that she is holding
out to him symbolises the protection
given to the deceased. In keeping
with conventions of two-dimensional
representation, the faces are shown
in profile while the eyes are frontal,
and the body combines the bust shown
frontally and the limbs in profile.

▼ MODEL OF A BOAT
Middle Kingdom,
12th dynasty, circa 1991-1928 BCE.
Tomb of Chancellor Nakhti at Assiut.
Wood and metal with polychrome, shell.
38.5 x 81 cm.

The tomb of Chancellor Nakhti yielded
not only an extraordinary wooden statue
of the deceased (also at the Louvre),
but also a large ensemble of funerary
furniture; In these early years of the
Middle Kingdom, it was the custom
to place small models representing
everyday activities in the tomb. They
were to accompany the deceased in
eternal life. Far from royal pomp, these
models evoke the humble life of ordinary
people, whose simplicity is also evoked
by their naive form, so far removed
from the royal style.

◀ **BODY OF A WOMAN,
PROBABLY NEFERTITI**
*New Kingdom, 18th dynasty,
reign of Amenophis IV-Akhenaten.
Quartzite, H. 29 cm.*

With its round belly and generous
thighs, this woman's body epitomises
the sensuality of Amarna art.
The pleats of the tunic, as rendered
in the red quartzite, subtly underline
the curves of the model, in keeping
with the canons of the style imposed
by Akhenaten, characterised by a
marked contrast between a narrow
bust and a generous lower belly.
It is generally agreed that this
headless statue represents Nefertiti,
wife of Amenophis IV.

▶ **KING AMENOPHIS IV**
*New Kingdom, 18th dynasty,
reign of Amenophis IV–Akhenaten
(1353–1337 BCE). Pillar fragment from
a building east of Karnak. Sandstone,
originally painted, 137 x 88 x 60 cm.*

Instantly recognisable by virtue of
his effeminate features, his almond
eyes and his fleshy lips, Amenophis IV
initiated a theological reform
combined with an artistic revolution.
Not only did the pharaoh, renaming
himself Akhenaten, radically
overhaul the Egyptian pantheon,
but he imposed new canons on
his artists. These are magnificently
illustrated by this fragment
of a colossus. Taken from a pillar
in a temple to the sun falcon
Re-Horakhty, its cartouche
hieroglypics refer to the name of
the god whose earthly incarnation
he considered himself to be.

▲ SARCOPHAGUS OF IMENEMINET
(interior, box and lid)
Third Intermediate Period, circa 1069–664 BCE.
Agglomerated, coated material, 187 x 48 cm.

The decoration of this sarcophagus is exclusively dedicated to Osiris, god of the dead, from whom it was believed the deceased would be granted resurrection. The emblems of the deity are distributed thus: on the back of the box, the Djed, symbolising the backbone of the god, who was honoured in Busiris (in Egyptian, Djedu), while on the lid and at the foot of the figure is a representation of the Abydos reliquary that held the god's head. Inside, the box is painted with scenes from the life of Osiris.

▶ PORTRAIT OF A WOMAN
Thebes, 2nd century CE. Limewood painted with encaustic, 33 x 20 cm.

Fixed on the mummy at face-height, this portrait offered an extraordinarily lifelike image of the deceased. The subtle brushwork renders the delicate complexion and tints the expression with a gentle melancholy. The same concern was at work in the rendering of the details, and especially the jewellery, a discreet allusion to the model's social status. Found, notably, in the Fayum region, works of this kind show how foreigners adopted Egyptian customs at the same time as locals borrowed from Roman art.

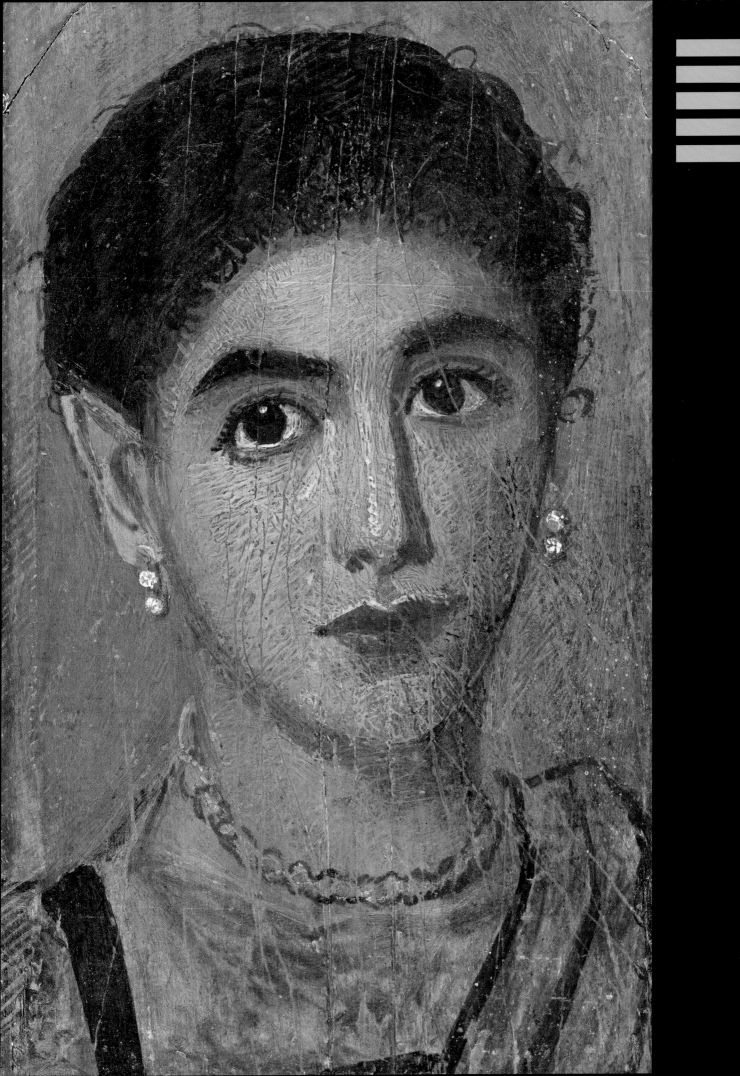

Greek, Etruscan and Roman Antiquities

The opening of the Musée du Louvre in the late eighteenth century coincided with the apogee of Neoclassicism and the taste for the antique. Theorised by writers such as Johann Joachim Winckelmann, the imitation of Greek and Roman works constituted the basis of all art that aspired to ideal beauty. Throughout their careers, painters and sculptors studied the statues collected by sovereigns, who vied with each other to obtain the most handsome vestiges of Antiquity. The Department of Greek, Etruscan and Roman Antiquities thus has its roots in the great French and Italian collections of the sixteenth to eighteenth centuries. Before Louis XIV, Richelieu and Mazarin amassed remarkable ensembles, but

the post-Revolutionary period marked a new, more active phase. The acquisition of the prestigious Borghese Collection in 1807, and then, after 1815, of part of the no less famous Albani Collection, brought into the Louvre some of the most famous antiquities, such as Hermaphroditos Asleep (p. 47). The first keeper of antiquities, Ennio Quirino Visconti, was the man behind this major enrichment. The nineteenth century also saw the arrival of the Venus de Milo (p. 44-45) and the Winged Victory of Samothrace (p. 43), and saw the scope of curatorial curiosity broaden to include Archaic Greece and Etruscan civilisation. The latter area was richly represented in the famous Campana Collection, acquired by

Napoleon III in 1861. This also comprised an extraordinary quantity of Greek ceramics, now displayed in the Galerie Campana. The refurbishment of the Salle du Manège (p. 10) in 2004 made it possible to exhibit, often for the first time, antiquities restored in the seventeenth or eighteenth century, and thus to highlight the close relationship of these modern artists to their models.   JEAN-FRANÇOIS LASNIER

▼ MALE TORSO, KNOWN AS THE 'MILETUS TORSO'

Cyclades, circa 480 BCE.
Marble, H. 132 cm.

Typifying the 'severe style', this fragment marks an essential phase that came between the hieratic quality of Archaic art and the balance of the Classical style. Following on from the tradition of kouroi, this sculpture attests the virtuosity of Greek artists in rendering human anatomy. While the posture is not totally natural, the powerful musculature is rendered with great fidelity. Made at the start of the fifth century BCE, this statue was reused in the second century BCE to decorate the theatre at Miletus, where it was found.

▶ HEAD OF A HORSEMAN, KNOWN AS THE 'RAMPIN HORSEMAN'

Athens, circa 550 BCE. Marble, traces of red and black paint, H. (head) 27 cm.

Found at the foot of the Acropolis, this head has been linked to fragments of a horseman found ten years earlier and kept in Greece, which have been cast for the Louvre. Long thought to be the effigy of a son of the tyrant Pisistrates, or of a Dioscuri, this statue more probably represents a victor at the Pan-Hellenic Games, as indicated by the crown of leaves on his forehead. The sculptor's art is brilliantly displayed in the ornamental refinement of the hair and its accessories, once heightened with red and black, and in the smiling portrayal of the model.

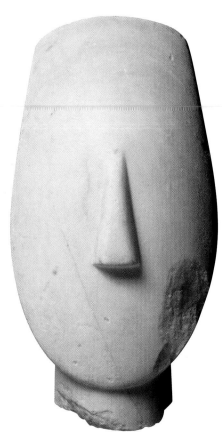

▲ HEAD OF A FEMALE STATUE

Cycladic culture, circa 2700-2300 BCE.
Marble, H. 27 cm.

This head belonged to a statue that was exhumed on the island of Keros. Nearly 1.5 metres high, it was exceptionally big for such a piece. The Early Bronze Age cradle of Greek sculpture, the Cycladic archipelago produced a great number of these enigmatic figures with their meticulously honed forms, incorrectly called 'idols'. In fact, their function and their meaning are still being debated because of the diversity of the contexts in which they were discovered.
Their immaculate whiteness, which is so alluring to the modern eye, was originally heightened with colour, especially on the eyes and mouth.

▼ KRATER, KNOWN AS THE 'BORGHESE VASE'
Athens (?), circa 40–30 BCE. Pentelicus marble,
H. 172 cm (including modern base), D. 135 cm.
Discovered in the Gardens of Sallust, Rome, in 1569.

Steeped in Hellenic culture, the Romans not only
copied ancient works, but also commissioned new
pieces from Greek sculptors. Athenian workshops in
the first century BCE also produced large quantities
of marble vases for Roman gardens. This vase, which
was found in Rome in the sixteenth century, adorned
the gardens of the Villa Borghese, where it was
considered one of the finest antiquities. Representing
Dionysus and Ariadne surrounded by maenads and
satyrs, it offers a synthesis of the different periods
of Greek art, which is characteristic of Hellenistic art.

▲ CALYX KRATER KNOWN AS THE 'NIOBIDES KRATER'
Attributed to the 'Niobides Painter', Athens,
circa 460-450 BCE. Terracotta, red-figure technique,
white highlights, H. 54 cm, D. 56 cm.
Provenance: Orvieto, Italy.

Developed in around 530 BCE, the technique
involving red figures on a black ground gave Attic
ceramists the capacity to achieve greater anatomical
and expressive precision. Using this technique, vase
painters were able to imitate the prestigious models
of mural painting, which today we know only
through this indirect echo. On one side of this vase
is a representation of the massacre of Niobe's
children by Apollo and Artemis, and on the other,
Heracles and Athena surrounded by heroes in arms.

▶ THE WINGED VICTORY OF SAMOTHRACE
Island of Samothrace, circa 190 BCE.
White Parian marble (statue) and grey Rhodes marble
(base), H. statue (with wings) 275 cm,
Total H. (with base) 557 cm.

Discovered in 1863 on the island of Samothrace,
in the northeastern corner of the Aegean Sea, by a
Frenchman, Charles Champoiseau, this statue had
been given to the sanctuary of the Cabeiri in
celebration of a victory, probably by the people of
Rhodes in the early second century BCE. Despite its
fragmentary state, the Victory is considered one of
the finest examples of Hellenistic art. The dynamic
posture of the figure seems to be redoubled by the
swirling drapery, that characteristic wet drapery
that reveals palpitating flesh as much as it covers it.

The Venus de Milo

Circa 130-100 BCE. Parian marble,
H. 211 cm. Discovered at Milo, Cyclades.

Admired, copied, quoted and
subverted, the Venus de Milo has
never ceased to fascinate the public
since it was brought to the Louvre
in 1821. Although world-famous, this
woman without any arms remains
paradoxically unknown. First of all,
she ought to be given her Greek
name 'Aphrodite de Melos'. Further,
given the absence of attributes,
her identification with the goddess
of love is itself debatable. We know
of many other mysteriously
fragmented statues, but none has
prompted such speculation.
Its discreet charm comes not so much
from the safely canonical Classical
face as from the soft, voluptuous
flesh conjured up by the sculptor's
chisel. The goddess seems to have
been caught at the moment her
garment is about to slide off, but is
clearly not making any sign
of modesty. Even more than in the
ancient iconography of Aphrodite
at her bath, this sculpture sets up
a subtle play between what is shown
and what is (for the moment) still
hidden. Organised around several
diverging diagonals, the statue
invites the beholder to take part
in that interplay, by moving slowly
round her.

▲ SARCOPHAGUS OF THE LEGEND OF ACTAEON
Circa 125-130 CE. Marble, 99 x 235 cm.
Found on the Via Labicana, near Rome.

In order to meet growing demand from
throughout the Roman Empire, sculptors of
sarcophagi began to adopt industrial principles:
the mythological figures required by the client
were thus fitted into standardised decorative
settings. Here, scenes showing Actaeon being
devoured by his dogs, in reference no doubt
to a violent death, are surrounded by rich
garlands supported by women with drapery
surmounted by a frieze with aquatic elements.

▼ 'SARCOPHAGUS OF THE SPOUSES'
Late sixth century BCE. Polychrome terracotta,
H. 114 cm, L. 194 cm. Found at Cerveteri, Italy.

A masterpiece of Etruscan art, the Sarcophagus
of the Spouses exemplifies the art of clay sculpture
that developed in Etruria, particularly in
architectural decoration. Designed to hold the
bodies or merely the ashes of the deceased,
it represents the patrons partaking of the funeral
banquet, at which various rituals were performed.
Although some of the colour has been lost
the work offers a moving and gracious image
of the union of the spouses in death.

▶ **ARTEMIS WITH A DOE,**
OR 'THE DIANA OF VERSAILLES'
Roman Imperial copy, first-second century CE.
Marble, H. 200 cm. Discovered in Italy (Nemi?).

A gift from Pope Paul IV to Henry II in 1556,
this figure of Artemis the hunter was the first large
statue to enter the king's collections, and was
always prominently displayed in royal palaces,
from Fontainebleau to Versailles and then the
Louvre. Sculpted in the first or second century ce,
this statue of Artemis imitates a model from the
fourth century BCE, as was common in Roman art
at the time. It was restored in 1602 by Barthélémy
Prieur, who modified the figure's physiognomy
and that of the animal, which was no doubt
originally a dog.

▼ **HERMAPHRODITOS ASLEEP**
Roman work of the Imperial period, second
century CE. Greek marble (Hermaphroditos)
and Carrara marble (mattress sculpted by Bernini
in 1619), 169 x 89 cm. Discovered in Rome
near the Baths of Diocletian.

Born of the loves of Hermes and Aphrodite,
Hermaphrodite, a young man of rare beauty, was
intensely desired by the nymph Salmacis, who
prevailed on Zeus to merge her body with his.
This myth inspired this sculpture of provocative
sensuality and clever ambiguity that needs
to be seen from two different vantage points to be
understood – just as Hermaphroditos had a double
nature. The prosaic reality of the male genitalia
shatters the idealised beauty of the female body.

Islamic Art

 Since the inauguration of the Louvre's first 'Muslim' room in 1905, the collections of Islamic art have grown steadily. Originally, from 1945 to 1993, they were part of the prestigious Department of Near Eastern Antiquities, which covered the territories of Mesopotamia, Iran, Central Asia, the Indus Valley and the Arabian Peninsula. With the opening of the Grand Louvre, Islamic arts from the seventh to the twentieth century were given their own rooms, housing works from Egypt, Moghul India, Ottoman Turkey, medieval Andalusia and North Africa. Finally, in 2010, four thousand pieces from the Musée des Arts Décoratifs will be added to the ten thousand listed items in the Louvre collection. Thus joined, the two collections will be able to compete with the two best collections in the West, those of the  Victoria and Albert Museum in London and the Metropolitan Museum in New York. Based in part on complementary gifts from the great Orientalist connoisseurs of the late nineteenth and early twentieth centuries, they will have recovered their unity. In the arts of ceramics, books, textiles, gold and silver and glass, the Louvre boats some unique, historic pieces, a number of them from former royal collections. These constitute the masterpieces of its Islamic arts section – or Department of Islamic Arts, as it has been known since August 2003. They include the Baptis-  tère [basin] of St. Louis (p. 51), the Pyxis of al-Mughira (p. 50) from classical Islam (eighth to fourteenth century), and the Peacock Dish (p. 52) from Ottoman Turkey (sixteenth to eighteenth century). And there are also some remarkable ensembles, notably the garden-carpets of Iran (p. 53), North India and Afghanistan (seventeenth and eighteenth centuries). Their presentation in specially designed spaces in the Cour Visconti will, for the first time, accord them due prominence in the museum.

DOMINIQUE BLANC

▲ PYXIS WITH THE NAME AL-MUGHIRA
*Spain, Madinat al-Zahra, 968. Elephant ivory,
carved and engraved decoration, H. 15 cm, D. 8 cm
(detail p. 48).*

This casket with its extremely complex
decoration was sculpted out of a single
elephant's tusk at the caliph's workshops in
Cordoba. This superbly balanced and elegant
composition features traditional princely
scenes of hunting and court life. In a multifoil
medallion a lutanist stands on a platform
supported by lions, flanked by a fan-bearer
and a drinker.

► CHARGER WITH CIRCLING FISH
*Iran, late thirteenth–early fourteenth century.
Siliceous clay, low-fire decoration and gold
on coloured opacified glaze, D. 35.7 cm.*

This dish is noteworthy for the sophistication
of its black, white and gold decoration edged with
red, applied over a pale green glaze. The theme
of wriggling fish around one central fish
(a symbol of the sun?) was common in Iran at this
time. The general aesthetic, the celadon colour,
the border of petals and the central fish, cast
in relief, are all borrowed from Chinese celadon
wares that were exported to the Islamic Orient.

► BASIN, KNOWN AS THE 'BAPTISTÈRE
OF SAINT LOUIS'
*Syria or Egypt, signed Mohammed ibn al-Zain,
late thirteenth–early fourteenth century.
Hammered bronze with gold, silver and niello inlay,
H. 23.5 cm, D. 50.5 cm.*

This basin, said to have been used as the
baptismal font of Louis XIII, is the finest piece
of silver and gold in the collection to have been
produced at the apogee of metalworking
in the Near East, in the thirteenth and fourteenth
centuries. It was made in the early years of the
Mamluk reign over Egypt and Syria, and consists
of a single sheet of bronze inlaid with wide
plaques of silver. Friezes of real or mythological
animals surround a central band depicting
a procession of court dignitaries, while princes
on horseback occupy the four roundels.

► INCENSE BURNER IN THE FORM OF A LION
*Iran, Khurasan, eleventh to twelfth century.
Bronze with openwork and engraving, inlaid with
glass paste (?), 28.2 x 32 cm.*

The Louvre's Islamic collections possess some
remarkably expressive animal bronzes with
practical uses. This lion is from a group
of seven pieces all characterised by their
protuberant fangs and similarly shaped ears
and noses. The head can be removed to place
the incense inside. The body and neck are
perforated to let out the perfume.

◀ **HORSE-HEAD DAGGER AND SCABBARD**
India, seventeenth century. Blade: steel, gold decoration; handle: rock crystal inlaid with gold, rubies and emeralds; scabbard: gold, engraved and dulled decoration, H. 50 cm.

The sumptuousness associated with Indian finery owes a great deal to the taste of the Moghul emperors (Akbar, Shah Jahan and Awrangzeb) for precious stones in the sixteenth to eighteenth centuries. Knives and swords made particularly fitting vehicles for their passion. Rock crystal handles made to fit the neck of a harnessed horse, decoration of emerald and ruby florets surrounded by gold filigree, and blades and scabbards in engraved, dulled metals reflected the refined taste of these great lovers of weapons and jewellery.

▲ **PEACOCK DISH**
Turkey, Iznik, 1540–55. Siliceous clay, decoration painted on white slip, transparent glaze, D. 37.5 cm.

The quintessence of the court art of Ottoman Turkey in the sixteenth and seventeenth centuries, the ceramics from the workshops of Iznik are represented in the Louvre in the form of big panels of colourful tiles and pieces of hollow ware. This dish stands out by virtue of its animal motif, which was rare in the sixteenth century, when Iznik raised the representation of plants to new heights of elegance and refinement. Derived from the world of books, the 'saz' style of drawing combines with a subtle graduation of blues on a white ground (a homage to China) in a supple, airy composition organised around the bird figure.

▶ **FRAGMENT OF A GARDEN CARPET, OR *CHAHÂRBÂGH***
Northwest Iran (Kurdistan), eighteenth century. Asymmetrical knotted stitch, wool, 256 x 130 cm.

Garden carpets were fashionable in India, Afghanistan and Iran. This one was made at the end of the Safavid dynasty, which marks the apogee of the Iranian carpet. It offers a view down onto a space organised according to the mirror principle. Fishy streams delimit the compartments and come together in the centre in octagonal basins framed by trees inhabited by singing birds. The figure eight is found in the branches of the stars, which figure beds of flowers in the 'heavenly garden' metaphor characteristic of Islamic carpets.

Sculptures

The Department of Sculptures offers a unique panorama of French sculpture from the Middle Ages to the nineteenth century. The opening of the Richelieu wing, articulated around the Puget and Marly courtyards, has made it possible to present this itinerary through the history of French art in all its richness. The collection can be divided up into several groups. First are the sculptures from Parisian churches that were saved during the Revolution, and the majority of these are of course religious – Virgins with Child, Christs on the Cross, bits of altarpieces, etc. But these works also include much funerary art, from the tomb of Philippe Pot to that of René de Birague by Germain Pilon. Next are the remarkable ensembles of sculptures from the royal residences and gardens at Versailles, Fontainebleau, Marly, Louveciennes, etc., an exemplary selection of which is displayed in the covered Marly and Puget courtyards, where the

dynamic forms of the spirited 'Marly Horses' and the power of Puget's Milo of Croton dominate. Civic sculpture is also represented, notably by vestiges from the monument built to glorify Louis XIV on Place des Victoires. Another category is formed by reception pieces, which were already kept in the Louvre back in the days when it housed the Royal Academy of Painting and Sculpture. These constitute some of the most interesting items in the collection: most French sculptors are represen-

ted here by an essential work from their career. And finally there are works from the yearly Salon, which replaced the Academy as an arena of artistic emulation in the eighteenth and nineteenth centuries. Rich highlights from these abundantly commented annual shows can be seen at the Louvre. In addition to French sculpture, the Department also has close links with Italy, and is actively developing its collection of Northern European works, especially from the Neoclassical period.

JEAN-FRANÇOIS LASNIER

◀ CHARLES V AND
JEANNE DE BOURBON
*Île de France, 1365–80,
Stone, H. 195 cm.*

With his wife Jeanne de Bourbon,
King Charles V continues to watch
over the destiny of the Louvre,
which owes him so much. He it was
who charged Raymond du Temple
with transforming the fortress built
by Philip Augustus into a true royal
residence. These two statues certainly
come from the exterior decoration
made for the palace at this time.
The sensitive observation and
truthfulness of the faces and clothes
reflect the rise of portraiture in the
second half of the fourteenth century.

◀ CHRIST REMOVED FROM THE CROSS
*Burgundy, 1365–80. Painted and gilded
maple wood, H. 155 cm.*

An effort of imagination is required
to picture this work with its original
colours, gilding and metal crown,
at the centre of a sculptural group
representing a *Descent from the Cross*.
But even bare and isolated, this statue
is deeply moving in its expressiveness.
The elongation of the figure and the
graphic treatment of the anatomy
transfigure Christ's body into a vivid
image of suffering. The inspiration
of this Burgundian artist manifests
clear kinship with that of the great
Romanesque portals of Vézelay
and Autun.

▼ TOMB OF PHILIPPE POT
*Burgundy, last quarter of fifteenth
century. Polychrome stone, H. 180 cm.*

After the fall of the Duchy of
Burgundy, the seneschal Philippe Pot
served the kings of France who now
governed the region. His tomb echoes
that of Philip the Bold, which is kept
in Dijon, but the small figures of
mourners on that sculpture have been
amplified to a human scale here.
Dressed in black, they carry the
deceased in his armour towards his last
resting place. This funeral procession
denotes the prestige of the seneschal
and his line. The tomb was originally
kept in the abbey of Cîteaux.

▶ DONATO DI NICCOLO BARDI, KNOWN AS DONATELLO
(CA. 1386–1466)
MADONNA AND CHILD
Relief, polychrome and gilded terracotta, 102 x 74 cm.

Donatello was the great renovator of sculpture in
Florence. Working in every material and genre,
he introduced a new naturalism into representations
of the figure, combined with references to Antiquity.
This naturalism is evident here in the colours of this
relief, but also in the postures and rendering of the
fabrics. As for the curtain in the background, it reminds
us of the work's illusionist dimension, while making
a discreet reference to the gold grounds of medieval art.

▶ GERMAIN PILON (ACTIVE 1540–1590)
MONUMENT OF THE HEART OF HENRY II
*1561–1566. The Three Graces (Germain Pilon)
with pedestal (Dominique Florentin).
Marble and gilded wood (vase), H. 255 cm.*

As both a man and a king by divine right, the French
sovereign had the privilege of resting for eternity in two
different places: his body in Saint-Denis, and his heart
in a place of his choosing: for Henry II this was the
Célestins church in Paris. Germain Pilon was charged
by the royal widow, Catherine de Médicis, with
sculpting the monument for the heart. On a pedestal
sculpted by Dominique Florentin in the Fontainebleau
style he placed the three Graces, ancient symbols
of conjugal fidelity, whose subtle elegance makes them
one of the masterpieces of French Mannerism.

▼ BENVENUTO CELLINI (1500–1572)
THE NYMPH OF FONTAINEBLEAU
1542–1543, high relief. Bronze, 205 x 409 cm.

Summoned to the court of France by Francis I,
the great Italian goldsmith and sculptor made this big
high relief for the main door (Porte Dorée) of the king's
château at Fontainebleau. In the end, however, the
work was installed at another residence, Anet.
This *Nymph* was Cellini's first monumental sculpture,
and presents an unsettling combination of power
and sensuality in an explicit homage to Michelangelo.
This contrast is echoed by the opposition between
the smooth, carefully polished flesh and the
scrupulous naturalism of the animal fleeces.

► GREGOR ERHART (1465–1540)
SAINT MARY MAGDALEN
1515. The church of the Dominicans in Augsburg (?).
Lime tree wood, polychromy. The low pedestal and forepart
of the feet were restored in the nineteenth century. H. 177 cm.

This statue of Mary Magdalen would originally have been
hung from the vault of a church, surrounded by a host of
angels leading her to heaven. It was therefore designed to
be seen from several different angles, which explains, for
example, the care taken with the way the hair falls down
the back. Covered only by her abundant red locks, the
saint's elegant, natural figure reveals a real concern with
corporeal beauty. This masterpiece attests the spreading
knowledge of Renaissance developments, which Albrecht
Dürer had helped disseminate in German-speaking lands.

MICHELANGELO BUONARROTI, KNOWN AS MICHELANGELO (1475–1564)

The Slaves

Rebellious Slave and Dying Slave 1513–15. Marble, H. 209 cm and 228 cm.

The destiny of Michelangelo's *Slaves* was a strange one: sculpted for the tomb of a pope, they reappeared on the façade of the Château d'Ecouen, then at the Château de Richelieu, before being transferred to the Louvre. With the *Slaves* of the Accademia in Florence and the statue of *Moses* in Rome, they are all that remains of a titanic project that failed to outlive its patron, Julius II. This pope, for whom Michelangelo worked on the ceiling of the Sistine Chapel, also asked him to sculpt his tomb in the basilica of Saint Peter's. The artist dreamed up a pyramidal structure decorated on every level with statues evoking the destiny of the soul. In this Neo-Platonic vision, the slaves were to symbolise the soul's imprisonment in the body. The incompleteness of the work parallels this struggle against matter, which both gave birth to he work and imprisoned it at the same time. The genius of Michelangelo is spectacularly manifest in the representation of the tensed human body; the power of the musculature is equalled only by the pathos of the expression.

▲ ANTONIO CANOVA (1757–1822)
PSYCHE REVIVED BY CUPID'S KISS
1787-93. Marble, H. 155 cm, W. 168 cm, D. 101 cm.

This is undoubtedly one of the most delicate
works by Antonio Canova, the uncontested
master of Neoclassical sculpture. Alongside
a register built on power and authority, Canova
also cultivated a style close to the refinement
of Mannerism. He loved, as here, to represent
adolescent bodies which he endowed with
sensuality and subtle ambiguity by carefully
polishing the marble and choosing graceful
postures. This sculpture was acquired
by General Murat, King of Naples, at the same
time as *Cupid and Psyche,* which is also
at the Louvre.

▶ GUILLAUME I COUSTOU (1677–1746)
**HORSE RESTRAINED BY A GROOM
(MARLY HORSE)**
1743-45. Marble, H. 355 cm.

In the effort of the grooms to control their
steeds, the 'Marly Horses' express man's eternal
struggle against untameable nature. The image
is extraordinarily vehement, quite devoid of
mythological allusions. Sculpted between 1743
and 1745 from a single block of marble, these
two groups replaced Coysevox's *Fame and
Mercury* in the park at Marly. Beyond the
technical tour de force, they marked the apogee
of a French Baroque tendency focused on the
expressive representation of vital forces.

... deurcix · Royne ꝺe france · et ꝺe Naue...

Decorative Arts

A temple to the genius of artisans and artists from the Early Middle Ages up to the Second Empire, the Department of Decorative Arts assembles all the different techniques with unusual exhaustiveness: tapestry, ceramics, glass and gold and silver, but also cabinet-making, horology, jewellery and sculpture. All kinds of different objects come together here in displays of stunning eclecticism: a bishop's crook and a king's sceptre, an ivory Virgin and a ceramic shepherd, a reliquary and a tobacco box. Sacred and profane cohabit harmoniously. The primary source of these very diverse collections are the churches and royal palaces whose treasures the museum inherited during the Revolu-

tion. The fabulous riches of Saint-Denis and the Sainte-Chapelle, even incomplete, meant a superb haul of gold and silver, of ivory and reliquaries and liturgical vestments, while the Crown residences (Versailles, Saint-Cloud, the Tuileries) brought the museum marquetry and lacquered commodes, sculpted wooden panelling, hangings woven with gold and silver and a complete range of chairs. The Louis XIV collection of gems, presented in the Galerie d'Apollon, constituted one of the most admired heritages of the Ancien Régime. In

the nineteenth and twentieth centuries, collectors contributed significantly to this ensemble, especially the superb bequests and donations made by the Rothschilds, David-Weills, Camondos and, most recently, Mme Grog-Carven. The opening of the Richelieu wing in 1993 marked a turning point in the history of the department by allowing it to present these riches on an unprecedented scale. The collection of tapestries, with the Hunts of Maximilian and History of Scipio hangings, are only the most spectacular part of this deployment.   JEAN-FRANÇOIS LASNIER

◀ PORPHYRY VASE: 'SUGER'S EAGLE'
Vase: Egypt or Imperial Rome;
mount: Saint-Denis before 1147. From the treasury
of the abbey of Saint-Denis.

Suger, the powerful abbot of Saint-Denis, believed
that in contemplating artistic treasures the believer
was bathed in divine light. For this reason he was
constantly enriching his abbey with precious
works, like this liturgical chalice, made by grafting
a virtuoso piece of medieval silver onto an ancient
object. Inspired by Byzantine and Oriental
models, 'Suger's Eagle' still has the characteristic
frontality of Romanesque art, while the naturalism
of the chiselled plumage already looks forward
to the Gothic.

◀ LEAF OF A DIPTYCH IN FIVE PARTS:
THE EMPEROR TRIUMPHANT (JUSTINIAN?)
Constantinople, first half of the sixth century.
Ivory, traces of inlay, 34.2 x 26.8 x 2.8 cm.

This leaf from a Byzantine diptych has come down
to us almost complete. Only one of the original
five plaques is missing. The others illustrate in
more or less allegorical fashion the triumph
of an emperor sometimes identified as Justinian
(527-565). In the centre, the sovereign on
horseback, sculpted in high relief, literally crushes
his enemy by sticking his lance in front of a Persian
or Scythian. On another plaque, a soldier presents
him with a statuette of Victory. The composition
is crowned by Christ in glory.

◀ SCEPTRE OF CHARLES V
Paris, 1364 (?). Gold, stones and pearls, H.: 60.5 cm.
From the treasury of the abbey of Saint-Denis.

Prepared by Charles V for the coronation of his
son, Charles VI, at Saint-Denis in 1380, this sceptre
enabled Charles V to legitimise the young Valois
dynasty, which had come to the throne half
a century earlier, by placing it under the authority
of Charlemagne. The Carolingian emperor appears
as a statuette and in three reliefs on the knob
illustrating episodes from his life. In these years
when Gothic was becoming an international style,
the art of gold and silver reached its apogee against
a backdrop of war, famine and epidemics.

▶ VIRGIN WITH CHILD
Paris, between 1324 and 1339.
Gilded silver, basse taille enamel on gilded silver,
stones and pearl, H. 69 cm (detail p. 64).

Presented by the wife of Charles IV to the abbey
of Saint-Denis in 1339, this work can be seen as
exemplary of the Parisian style of the first half
of the fourteenth century, with its elegant S-shaped
silhouette, drapery and the fullness of the face. The
gentle, melancholy expression is also typical. In her
hand, the figure holds a reliquary lily supposed to
contain the clothes, hair and milk of the Virgin.
On the pedestal, scenes from the life of Christ are
represented in translucent basse-taille enamelwork.

▶ LÉONARD LIMOSIN (CIRCA 1505–CIRCA 1576)
PORTRAIT OF HIGH CONSTABLE
ANNE DE MONTMORENCY

Limoges, 1556. Painted enamel on copper
with giltwood mount, 72 x 56 cm (with mount).

Invented by the ceramists of Limoges, painted enamel
can be seen as one of the most original and accomplished
techniques of the Renaissance, when it achieved
a perfection that has never been equalled. Vying with
painters, the enamellers, of whom Léonard Limosin was
the uncontested master, took on the great subjects
of religious and mythological painting, but also portraits.
The ornamental repertoire, which is typical of the
Fontainebleau School, shows the development
and supremacy of pictorial models in the decorative arts.

◀ TAPESTRY OF THE HUNTS OF MAXIMILIAN:
THE MONTH OF JULY (LEO)
Brussels, 1531–33, after Bernard Van Orley.
Wool, silk, gold and silver, 430 x 570 cm.

At the start of the sixteenth century, the Brussels tapestry
workshops achieved uncontested supremacy by transposing
models provided by the greatest painters into tapestry.
Bernard Van Orley produced the cartoons for the hanging
of the 'Hunts of Maximilian'. Each piece represents
a month of the year and is symbolised by a sign of the
zodiac and a seasonal hunting scene. The tapestry makers
have faithfully rendered the details and nuances of the
pictorial model. Golden and silver threads give the work
a sumptuary quality.

▲ ANDRÉ-CHARLES BOULLE (1642-1732)
WARDROBE 'WITH PARROT'
Paris, circa 1700. Oak with ebony and amaranth veneer,
polychrome wood marquetry, brass, pewter, tortoiseshell,
horn, gilt bronze, 255 x 157 x 58 cm.

This wardrobe provides dazzling proof of the genius
of cabinetmaker André-Charles Boulle and his contribution
to the decorative arts in the reign of Louis XIV. He was
one of the first to create single-chest wardrobes with two
doors, thus giving the object a monumentality that he
underscored with gilt bronze. This wardrobe also features
tableaux in wood marquetry on a tortoiseshell ground and
decorative friezes and panels combining pewter and brass,
also on a tortoiseshell ground. This technique was
henceforth known by his name.

▶ EWER IN SARDONYX
First century BCE/first century CE;
mount: Pierre Delabarre, Paris, circa 1630.
Enamelled gold, rubies, 27.5 x 16.5 cm.

Louis XIV was a passionate collector who
assembled a dazzling collection of hardstone
or 'gem' vases antiques. Agate, sardonyx,
jasper, lapis-lazuli, amethyst and rock crystal
were set in often extravagantly wrought
mounts of gold and silver. Pierre Delabarre
was one of the masters of this art, manifesting
a taste for fantastical ornaments (dragons, etc.)
with polychrome enamel shimmering around
coloured stones. This ewer has been on show
in the Galerie d'Apollon ever since 1861.

▶ TIARA OF EMPRESS EUGÉNIE
Gabriel Lemonnier, jeweller, Paris 1853.
212 pearls, 1,998 diamonds, silver lined with
gold, H. 7 cm, W. 19 cm, D. 18.5 cm.

Sold in 1887 with the Crown Diamonds,
this tiara was part of a set of jewellery
commissioned for Empress Eugénie
by Napoleon III after their wedding. By a
historical irony, the jeweller, Lemonnier, made
it by reusing pearls and diamonds from
a parure made by Nitot for Marie-Louise,
wife of Napoleon I.

▶ THE 'REGENT' DIAMOND
140.64 carats.

Discovered in India in 1698, this diamond
was cut in England between 1704 and 1706.
At the time it was considered the finest stone
in the world, because of both its purity
and the quality of the brilliant cut. Acquired
by Philippe d'Orléans in 1717, it became the
favoured ornament of royal power.
The 'Regent' thus adorned the crowns of most
French sovereigns up to Napoleon III.
Louis XV and Louis XVI also used to wear
it on their hat, while Napoleon Bonaparte
had it set into his sword.

▶ NECKLACE AND EARRINGS
OF THE EMPRESS MARIE-LOUISE
François-Regnault Nitot, jeweller, Paris, 1810.
Necklace: 32 emeralds, 1,138 diamonds,
gold, silver; earrings: 6 emeralds, 108 diamonds,
gold, silver.

On the occasion of his wedding in 1810,
Napoleon I offered the new empress,
Marie-Louise of Austria, this superb parure,
which also included a tiara and a comb.
For the necklace alone, jeweller François-
Regnault Nitot used 32 emeralds and more
than a thousand diamonds. In 1814,
Marie-Louise retained possession of her
personal jewellery, which she later bequeathed
to the Grand Duke of Tuscany, Leopold II.

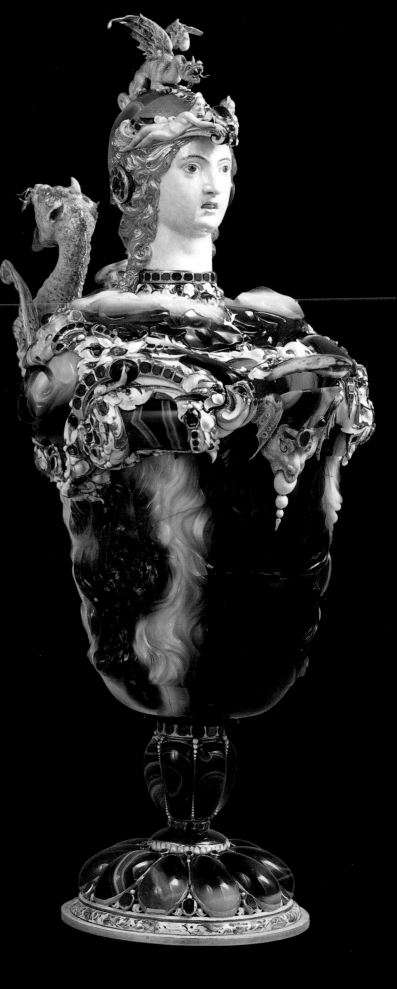

Paintings

With over six thousand paintings, from the late thirteenth to the mid-nineteenth century, presented by national school ever since the opening of the museum in 1793, the Louvre proclaims its encyclopaedic aspirations. Not surprisingly, the French School takes pride of place, with nearly two thirds of the collections, followed by the Italian and Flemish. The core of the museum was formed by former royal collections. Francis I amassed treasures of Italian painting (Leonardo da Vinci, Raphael, Titian), and Louis XIV bought up whole collections, such as those of Cardinal Mazarin and the banker from Cologne, Everhard Jabach. The Sun King was also the great champion of Classicism. It is to him that the museum owes its outstanding ensembles of work by Nicolas Poussin, Claude Lorrain and Charles Le Brun. And with the foundation of the Royal Academy of Painting in

1648, the Crown was regularly enriched by the commissioned work of its own Academicians. Through to the nineteenth century, the state played an important role by issuing public commissions that helped, notably, to reinvigorate the art of history painting. The creation in 1818 of the Musée du Luxembourg, dedicated to living artists, made it possible to acquire modern paintings (Géricault, Delacroix). But the museum also grew as a result of events both political and artistic, from revolutionary requisitions and war booty as well as donations and purchases. The La Caze Collection, donated in 1869, thus filled major gaps in the seventeenth century (Le Nain and the painters of social reality) and eighteenth century (Watteau, Chardin, Frago-

nard). The creation of the different collections was also linked to changes in taste. Napoleon III's purchase of the Campana Collection in 1861, for example, reflected the vogue for the Italian Primitives (Paolo Uccello, Cosmè Tura), who had never been fashionable before. The interest in Spain developed only in the Romantic period, while it was not until the Anglomanie of the 1900s that the first big English portraits were hung on the museum walls.

MANUEL JOVER

▲ ENGUERRAND QUARTON
(ACTIVE IN PROVENCE FROM 1444 TO 1466)
**THE PIETÀ OF VILLENEUVE-
LÈS-AVIGNON**
Circa 1455.
Oil on wood panel, 163 x 218 cm.

This is a prime example of the kind
of art that developed in Avignon
during the fifteenth century under
the influence of the Netherlandish
painters. The presumed artist,
Enguerrand Quarton, combines stark
realism (the face of the donor,
the stiff corpse of Christ) with the
austere clarity of monumental forms
against a black ground and gold sky.

▶ JEAN COUSIN *LE PÈRE* (CIRCA 1490–1560)
EVA PRIMA PANDORA
Circa 1550.
Oil on wood panel, 97 x 150 cm.

Jean Cousin was for many years
an almost mythical artist, and even
today it is hard to determine his body
of work: this in fact is the only
painting that can be attributed to him
with any certainty. The elongated
forms of the body and the cold,
precious colours recall the artistic
style developed in Fontainebleau
in the reign of Francis I. The subject
is a singular one: Eve is presented
as a first Pandora, at the moment
when the vases from which all the ills
and benefits of humanity will spring
forth are still closed.

▶ SCHOOL OF FONTAINEBLEAU
**GABRIELLE D'ESTRÉES AND
ONE OF HER SISTERS**
Circa 1594.
Oil on wood panel, 96 x 125 cm.

The artists of the 'Second School
of Fontainebleau' (second half
of the sixteenth century) frequently
painted women at their toilet.
This fascinating painting represents
Gabrielle d'Estrées, the favourite
of Henry IV, taking a bath with her
sister, the Duchesse de Villars, who
is shown pinching her breast. Rather
than some playful gesture, this
is probably an allusion to the birth
of the king's natural child.

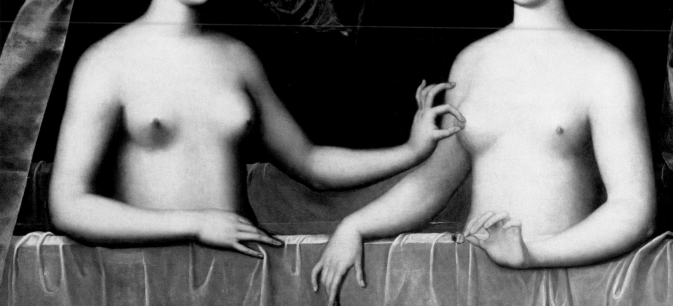

▲ JEAN CLOUET (1485/90–1541)
PORTRAIT OF FRANCIS I,
KING OF FRANCE (1494–1547)
Circa 1530. Oil on wood panel, 96 x 74 cm.

In this age which saw the formation of
centralised kingdoms, royal portraiture broke
with the realism of the previous period. From
now on, ceremonial portraits would present
an idealised image of the sovereign. Portraits
of Francis I thus always exhibit a young,
smiling and flattering image. Here, the king's
physical vitality is underscored by the richness
of his Italian-style clothing.

▶ HYACINTHE RIGAUD (1659–1743)
LOUIS XIV (1638–1715)
1701. Oil on canvas, 277 x 194 cm.

This painting commissioned in 1701, initially
for Philip V of Spain, offers the most striking
formulation of the 'state portrait'. The king
as real person almost entirely disappears behind
the fictive body that serves as the archetype
of the 'handsome prince' in accordance with
the canons of the day. The body and the
insignia of power that extend it (the ermine-
lined coat of fleurs-de-lis, the crown, the
'Joyous' sword, the sceptre, and the hand of
justice) affirm the majesty and pomp deemed
meet for the expression of absolutism.

The Card Sharp

Circa 1635. Oil on canvas, 106 x 146 cm.

Rediscovered in the twentieth century after years of neglect, the work of Georges de La Tour represents one of the finest comeback stories in the history of art. This painter from Lorraine is famous today for his wonderful 'night paintings' steeped in an atmosphere of silent meditation, but he is also a painter of 'diurnal' scenes that are just as extraordinary. As in the famous Caravaggio painting, the idea of which La Tour makes his own here, the card sharp is cheating with the cards behind his back. Facing him is the poor fool who is about to be duped. In the middle, the luxuriously dressed dowager is clearly not innocent: her sidelong glance at the servant in the turban gives their game away. The painter has captured the relations between the characters with compelling acuity. His art dazzles by the beauty of its light and colours, its rendering of materials, the purity of its forms and the liveliness of the detail.

◀ CLAUDE GELLÉE, KNOWN AS LE LORRAIN OR CLAUDE (1600–1682)
CLEOPATRA DISEMBARKING AT TARSUS
1642–43,
Oil on canvas, 119 x 168 cm.

Claude Gellée, known in France as Lorrain, after his native Duchy, spent most of his career in Rome, where his landscapes were hugely popular. He specialised in views of imaginary harbours with real or imaginary Antique architecture. These enchanting settings were often the backdrop for scenes taken from ancient history, acted out by figures on a very small scale. With Poussin, Lorrain was one of the great inventors of the Classical landscape. His views are poetical idealisations of nature, but they are based on acute observation of the play of sunlight, something he shared with the Northern European school of landscape.

◀ NICOLAS POUSSIN (1594–1665)
THE SHEPHERDS OF ARCADIA, ALSO KNOWN AS 'ET IN ARCADIA EGO'
Circa 1638–40.
Oil on canvas, 85 x 121 cm.

The Louvre has thirty-nine paintings by Poussin, nearly all of them from royal collections. This fact reflects the eminence enjoyed throughout the centuries by this artist who was seen as the quintessence of a national aesthetic: Classicism. This painting epitomises Poussin's meticulously conceived art, in which all the elements are articulated in accordance with the philosophical implications of the subject. The kneeling shepherd reads the Latin inscription engraved on the tomb: 'Et in Arcadia ego', meaning that even in the happy land of Arcadia, death is present. The beholder is thus invited to 'read' the painting and meditate on the thought it conveys.

▼ NICOLAS POUSSIN
THE RAPE OF THE SABINE WOMEN
Circa 1637–38.
Oil on canvas, 159 x 206 cm.

Applying to painting a system of categories based on knowledge of ancient music, Poussin varied his expressive register in accordance with the 'mode' he deemed appropriate to the nature of the subject. Where his *Shepherds of Arcadia* is elegiac in tone, here the painter adopted the 'Phrygian' mode, which was 'vehement, furious and very severe', and which suited 'dreadful war themes'. The subject is taken from ancient history: here, the Romans carry away the Sabine women in order to make them their wives.

◄ JEAN-ANTOINE WATTEAU (1684–1721)
PIERROT, FORMERLY KNOWN AS GILLES
Circa 1718–19. Oil on canvas, 185 x 150 cm.

This painting is one of the great eighteenth-century masterpieces that entered the Louvre as part of the La Caze Collection. Its size, exceptional for Watteau, suggests that he may have painted it as a sign for his friend Belloni, a former actor who had opened a café. The figures are all from Commedia dell'Arte, which was in vogue in Paris at the time: Pierrot (centre), the doctor, the lovers Leander and Isabella, and (in the background) the captain. But none of this explains the strangely moving effect of this wistful, clownish figure drowning in his white costume.

▲ JEAN-ANTOINE WATTEAU
PILGRIMAGE TO CYTHERA
1717. Oil on canvas, 129 x 194 cm.

Gathering around the statue of Venus, lovers make ready to board the vessel that will carry them to Cythera, the island of Love. In this canvas, which was his reception piece for the Academy in 1712, Watteau gives a mythological inflection to what is the central theme of all his work: the *fête galante*, that theatre of love's quest in which frivolity is often tinged with a subtle melancholy.

► FRANÇOIS BOUCHER (1703–1770)
DIANA LEAVING HER BATH
1742. Oil on canvas, 57 x 73 cm.

Boucher, the master of Rococo art and favourite of the Marquise de Pompadour, was at his best in mythological scenes showcasing delectably undressed ladies. Here, the shimmering colours, with nacreous pinks and almond greens, create an atmosphere of erotic enchantment. Diana and her companion have just emerged from their bath after a successful hunt. The quiver full of arrows, the dogs and the game are the customary attributes of the goddess.

▼ Jean-Siméon Chardin (1699–1779)
The Skate
1728. Oil on canvas, 114 x 146 cm.

Chardin was essentially a painter of still
lifes and genre scenes, which were both
relatively low in the hierarchy of genres.
This, however, did not keep him from
gaining entry into the Academy the very
day this painting was displayed.
Its qualities were praised as worthy of
the finest Flemish painters, to which the
painting does indeed refer. The rendering
of the textures and the subtlety of
the colour, especially in the gutted skate,
combine to produce the pictorial
'magic' that was acclaimed by Diderot.

◀ ÉLISABETH VIGÉE-LEBRUN (1755-1842)
**MADAME VIGÉE-LEBRUN
AND HER DAUGHTER**
1789. Oil on wood, 130 x 94 cm.

This artist was one of the preferred
portraitists of Marie-Antoinette. Fleeing
the Revolution, she travelled around
Europe, meeting with tremendous
success thanks to the natural poses,
unaffected grace and sensitive expression
that were the hallmarks of her work.
Vigée-Lebrun painted herself a number
of times, holding her daughter in her
arms. While the tender and effusive
quality of this portrait bespeaks the cult
of sensibility, the antique-style clothing
denotes Neoclassical tastes.

▼ JEAN-HONORÉ FRAGONARD (1732–1806)
THE BOLT
Circa 1777. Oil on canvas, 74 x 94 cm.

Fragonard is famous, among other
things, for his witty and lively renderings
of saucy themes, a bit like visual one-
liners. Starting in 1775, he developed
a new manner, with a smooth, glossy
finish. *The Bolt* is the outstanding
example of this. The scene is explicit
enough not to need explanations and,
as art historian Daniel Arasse pointed
out, the chaos and suggestive shapes of
the bed offer ample visual commentary
on the lovemaking to come.

The Coronation of the Emperor Napoleon I

Paris, 1806–07. Oil on canvas, 621 x 979 cm.

As official painter to the Emperor, it fell to David to commemorate the coronation ceremony held on 2 December 1804 in Notre-Dame de Paris. Initially, David showed Napoleon in the process of crowning himself, which is what actually happened. But since this action was considered too provocative, he decided to illustrate the moment when the Emperor crowned Josephine, in front of (a critical) Pius VII, who gave his blessing, and over a hundred other figures. To the left stand the princesses and Napoleon's sisters and sisters-in-law; in the centre, in the tribune, sits Madame Mère, Napoleon's mother, who in reality was absent; below her, Murat and the other marshals in feathered hats; in the foreground, to the right, political dignitaries carrying the insignia of power (sceptre, hand of justice, globe). The consecration is at once a fascinating history painting and a gigantic portrait gallery. And it pleased the Emperor: 'It is not painting, for this is a picture one walks around in', he is reported to have said when he saw the finished work.

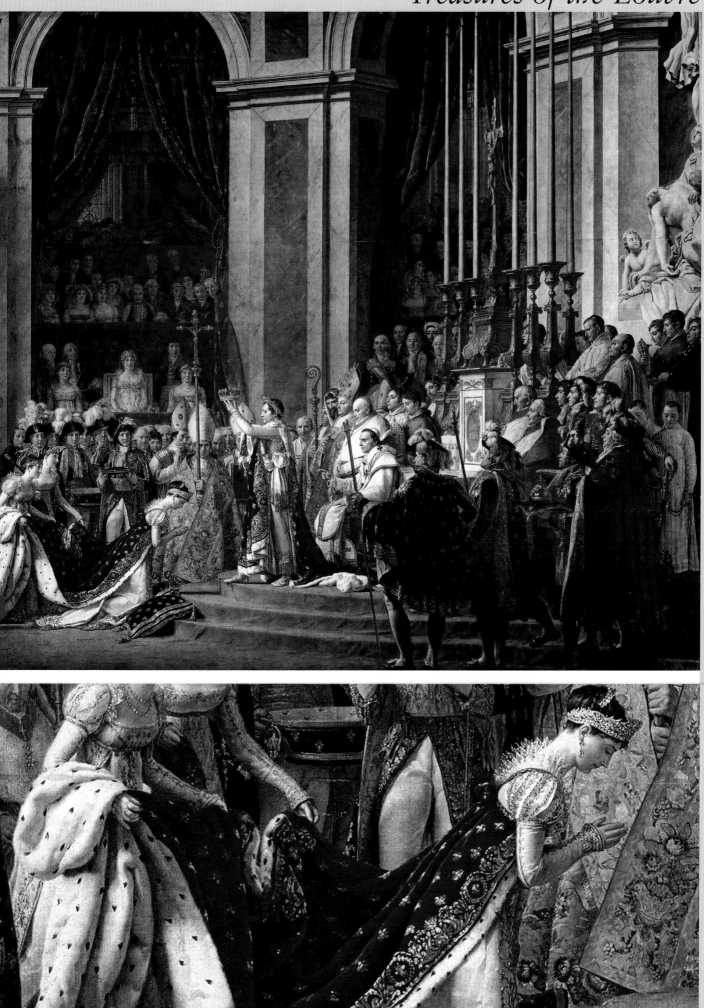

▲ Théodore Géricault (1791–1824)
The Raft of the Medusa
1819. Oil on canvas, 491 x 716 cm.

Because it gave a politically fraught event the full-blown epic dimensions of history painting, this work caused a sensation at the Salon of 1819. It evokes the tragic plight of the survivors of the wrecked *Medusa*, who drifted over the seas on a raft for twelve days in 1816, and captures the moment when they spotted the ship that would rescue them. This sensitivity to contemporary events was a prominent feature of early Romantic art in the aftermath of the Empire.

▶ Eugène Delacroix (1798–1863)
**Liberty Leading the People
(28 July 1830)**
1831. Oil on canvas, 260 x 325 cm.

During the 'Three Glorious Days' of 1830, the people of Paris rose up against the autocratic regime of Charles X and built barricades throughout the capital. Delacroix commemorated the event with a combination of allegory (Liberty brandishing the tricolour flag) and tragic realism (the corpses).

▲ EUGÈNE DELACROIX (1798–1863)
THE DEATH OF SARDANAPALUS
1827. Oil on canvas, 392 x 496 cm.

This great 'poem' of flesh, fire and blood, lit up by the flash of gold, jewellery and fabrics, marks the apogee of French Romantic painting. It attests the fascination of a mythical Orient for the painters of Delacroix's generation. The subject is taken from a tragedy of the same name by the poet Byron: seeing herself surrounded by his enemies, the king of Nineveh had his wives, slaves and horses killed and then set light to the pyre from which he had contemplated the massacre.

▶ CAMILLE COROT (1796–1875)
**RECOLLECTION
OF MORTEFONTAINE**
1864. Oil on canvas, 65 x 89 cm.

Delacroix acclaimed Corot as the 'father of the modern landscape'. The evolution of his style after 1850 brought him long-awaited success. The landscapes he painted at Ville d'Avray, southwest of Paris, often represent the park and pond at Mortefontaine in misty, silvery hues that make the image evoke memory rather than an actual view.

▶ JEAN-AUGUSTE-DOMINIQUE INGRES (1780–1867)
UNE ODALISQUE
1814. Oil on canvas, 91 x 162 cm.

In contrast to the turbulence of Romantic art, Ingres was the great representative and renewer of Classicism. He referred to nature, Raphael and Antiquity, while subjecting the canons of ideal beauty to a series of anatomical distortions. This Odalisque has been subjected to rigorous formal constraints: the back, arm and fingers were elongated, the breasts displaced and the modelling attenuated in order to create a self-sufficient harmony of forms and lines.

▲ GUIDO DI PIETRO, KNOWN AS FRA ANGELICO
(ACTIVE IN FLORENCE IN 1417–1455)
THE CORONATION OF THE VIRGIN
Circa 1430–32. Tempera on wood panel, 209 x 206 cm.

According to legend, 'Beato' Angelico saw celestial
figures in dreams and then depicted them in paint.
Certainly, with their lambent, radiant colours, his figures
do seem to exist in some supra-terrestrial world.
This Dominican monk had a deeply religious conception
of painting. His art reflects a sensibility that is still
medieval, but has assimilated the rational, realist space
elaborated in Florence at the start of the Quattrocento.

▶ PAOLO DI DONO, KNOWN AS UCCELLO (1397–1475)
THE BATTLE OF SAN ROMANO (THE COUNTERATTACK
BY MICHELETTO DA COTIGNOLA)
Circa 1435–40. Tempera on wood panel, 183 x 317 cm.

This is one of the three panels commissioned by
Cosimo de' Medici to commemorate the victory of the
Florentines over the Siennese at San Romano in 1432.
Uccello's work still manifests the Gothic attachment
to ornamental splendour, achieved here in the helmets
and armour, bridles and flags. At the same time, his
fascination with perspective leads to all kinds of virtuoso
foreshortenings and geometrical forms, resulting
in a space that is at once turbulent and constrained,
and whose strangeness fascinated the moderns.

ANDREA MANTEGNA (1431–1506)
SAINT SEBASTIAN
Circa 1480. Tempera on canvas, 255 x 140 cm.

More than any other artist, Mantegna embodies
the passion for Antiquity that was one of the
driving forces of the Italian Renaissance. Note
the archaeological precision with which each
column, capital, pillar and entablature of the
Roman temple here is depicted. The architecture
of the human body is similarly thorough. Artists
were now truly familiar with anatomical reality.

▲ DOMENICO GHIRLANDAIO (1449–1494)
OLD MAN WITH A YOUNG BOY
Circa 1490. Tempera on wood, 62 x 46 cm.

The models for this touching painting may
have been Francesco Sassetti, the director
of the Medici bank, and his grandson.
The exchange of looks between the old
man afflicted by a disfiguring illness
and the child snuggling up in his arms
creates an atmosphere of tenderness.
But this confrontation between old age and
childhood can also be read as an allegory:
the winding road in the landscape behind
evokes the path of life.

◀ RAFFAELLO SANTI, KNOWN AS RAPHAEL
(1483–1520)
**VIRGIN AND CHILD WITH THE YOUNG
SAINT JOHN THE BAPTIST,
KNOWN AS 'LA BELLA GIARDINIERA'**
Circa 1507. Oil on wood panel, 122 x 80 cm.

Of all the Madonnas painted by Raphael,
this is rightfully one of the most famous.
It dates from the artist's Florentine period,
from 1504 to 1508, when his style bloomed
in contact with the art of Michelangelo ect
balance of the pyramidal composition,
the fullness of the forms, the serenity of the
postures and expressions and their harmony
with the limpid landscape all make this
work emblematic of Renaissance classicism
at its apogee.

▼ TIZIANO VECELLIO, KNOWN AS TITIAN
(1488/90–1576)
THE PASTORAL CONCERT
Circa 1509. Oil on canvas, 105 x 137 cm.

Long attributed to Giorgione, this painting
is now credited to his student, Titian.
A 'pastoral' with complex allegorical meanings,
its central theme is music, a symbol of universal
harmony. In a verdant setting illuminated by the
dramatic light of sunset, two young musicians
are accompanied by two nymphs, who are
invisible to them. The combination of nude and
landscape, the musical theme and the sensuality
of the light and colour are constants in Venetian
Renaissance painting.

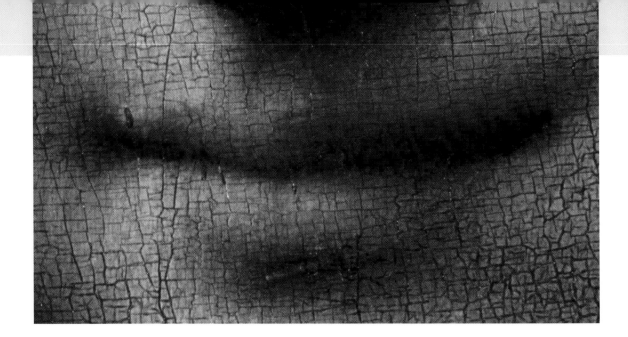

LEONARDO DA VINCI (1452–1519)

Mona Lisa

Circa 1503–06. Oil on wood, 77 x 53 cm.

The most famous painting in the world seems set to keep its mystery. The likely model of this portrait is known: she is thought to be Lisa, wife of Francesco del Giocondo. Since *gioconda* means 'joyous', it would seem that her name determined the sitter's smiling expression, and the painting's familiar name, the *Gioconda* (in Italian, *Joconde* in French). However, the mystery does not lie in the model's identity, but in the endlessly suggestive qualities of da Vinci's painting: the suggestiveness of the light and shadow, that melt into and shade each other, making the forms elusive; the suggestion of a soul that seems to be movingly manifested in the face; and the suggestion of a time that is both present and immemorial. The young woman poses like a guardian in front of a strange and wild land of mountains and glaciers, evoking the beginning of the world. The human person and her cosmic background both seem part of a sequence of mysterious phenomena that painting has the capacity to make visible, providing that it endows itself with 'magnetic' powers.

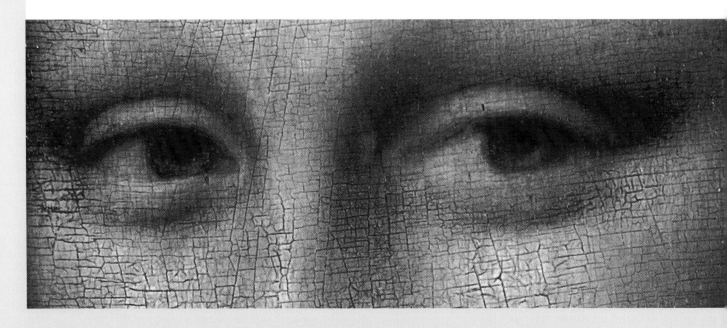

▶ TIZIANO VECELLIO, KNOWN AS TITIAN
(1488/90–1576)
WOMAN WITH TWO MIRRORS
1512-15. Oil on canvas, 99 x 76 cm.

Titian painted a series of beautiful
women, depicted at mid-height and
in a greater or lesser degree of undress,
which may or may not be idealised
portraits, genre scenes or allegories.
Here, a young woman is shown at her
toilet, accompanied by her lover.
A superb colourist, Titian concentrated
the sensuality of his subject in the
voluptuous harmony of the flesh,
the open white blouse and the red hair.

◀ LEONARDO DA VINCI (1452–1519)
**THE VIRGIN AND CHILD
WITH SAINT ANNE**
Circa 1510. Oil on wood, 168 x 130 cm.

This is Leonardo da Vinci's most
famous work after the *Mona Lisa*.
The two paintings have a lot of features
in common: the impalpable smiles that
express the joy of the soul, the
perfection of the *sfumato* that blurs
contours and makes the forms melt into
their shadow, and their imaginary
landscapes, which encapsulate the
artist's experiments with atmospheric
perspective.

▶ MICHELANGELO MERISI,
KNOWN AS CARAVAGE (1571-1610)
THE DEATH OF THE VIRGIN
*1601-1605/06,
Oil on canvas, 369 x 245 cm.*

Caravaggio started an artistic
revolution by introducing ordinary
working men and women and everyday
life into his religious paintings, thus
injecting human drama and immediacy
into holy scenes. Here, the Virgin
is painted as a corpse with a swollen
belly, and the apostles are wretches
burdened with grief. There is no
decorum, no angels in the heavens:
the event becomes an inner experience.
This 'scandalous' work was rejected
by those who commissioned it.

PAOLO CALIARI, KNOWN
AS VERONESE (1528–1588)
**THE WEDDING FEAST
AT CANA**
1562–63,
Oil on canvas, 677 x 994 cm.

In this gigantic painting
– the biggest in the Louvre –
Veronese displays his dazzling
talents as a decorative painter.
The Biblical scene has been
transposed into a magnificent
Venetian palace where a
sumptuous banquet is being
given. Around Christ and Mary,
at the centre, the artist has
distributed a host of figures
wearing the costume of his day,
including his own person,
along with his friends Titian,
Tintoretto, Bassano
and Palladio, in the group
of musicians at the front
of the scene.

▶ ALBRECHT DÜRER (1471–1528)
**PORTRAIT OF THE ARTIST
HOLDING A THISTLE**
*1493. Oil on parchment on canvas,
56.5 x 44.5 cm.*

This is the only Dürer painting in any
French museum. The artist was
twenty-two when he painted this first
self-portrait. He was about to marry,
so the thistle in his hand may
symbolise conjugal fidelity. It could
also be an allusion to the Passion,
as suggested by the inscription beside
the date: 'Things happen to me as
it is written on high'.

◀ JAN VAN EYCK (1390/95–1441)
THE VIRGIN OF CHANCELLOR ROLIN
Circa 1435. Oil on panel, 66 x 62 cm.

The donor, Nicolas Rolin, was the
chancellor of Philip the Good. He had
himself depicted praying before
the Virgin with Child, who is being
crowned by an angel. Behind this
main scene, the pictorial space spreads
through a flowering garden and
on into a sweeping river landscape
reaching all the way to the horizon.
A master of painting in oils, Van Eyck
gave his representations a degree
of realism never seen before him.
But this realism is itself transcended by
the transparent brilliance of his light.

▶ QUENTIN METSYS (1465–1530)
THE MONEYLENDER AND HIS WIFE
1514. Oil on board, 71 x 68 cm.

This panel derives from a lost
prototype by Jan Van Eyck, whose
style is echoed in the meticulous
rendering of the details and in the use
of the convex mirror to reflect
the space outside the depicted scene.
The missal read by the woman,
the scales held by the lender, alluding
to the weighing of souls at the Last
Judgement, betray the moralising
message of this genre scene.

◀ PETRUS PAULUS RUBENS (1577–1640)
**MARIE DE MÉDICIS LANDING
IN MARSEILLE, 3 NOVEMBER 1600**
1622–25. Oil on canvas, 394 x 295 cm.

The Louvre possesses one of the finest
ensembles of Rubens paintings anywhere
in the world, a notable highlight of which
is the cycle devoted to Marie de Médicis,
which originally constituted the decorative
painting for the Palais du Luxembourg.
These twenty-four huge canvases celebrating
the life of the queen are a summit of
Baroque art. Historical events are treated
allegorically, with a grandeur and
magnificence that dazzled contemporaries.
Here, in the foreground, sea divinities rejoice
at the queen's arrival in Marseilles harbour.

▶ REMBRANDT, HARMENSZ VAN RIJN (1606–1669)
BATHSHEBA AT HER BATH
1654. Oil on canvas, 142 x 142 cm.

When he represented the human body,
Rembrandt kept faith with the Northern
European tradition, which rejected the
idealisation advocated by the Italians.
He did not paint 'nudes' but naked human
beings. Thus Bathsheba, having read
the letter from King David who lusts after
her and wants her to be his, appears in all
the splendour of her vulnerable flesh, lit up
by the melancholy of her saddened soul.

▶ JOHANNES VERMEER (1632-1675)
THE ASTRONOMER, OR THE ASTROLOGIST
1668. Oil on canvas, 51 x 45 cm.

The astronomer has put aside his reading
of a treatise (identified by specialists as
'On the Study or Observation of the Stars')
to examine the heavenly globe. In an age
when Copernicus's heliocentric system was
recognised, when scientists already had
telescopes and microscopes, rational
knowledge was replacing the magical
interpretation of nature. As for the painter,
he dedicated himself to studying the unifying
principle of light.

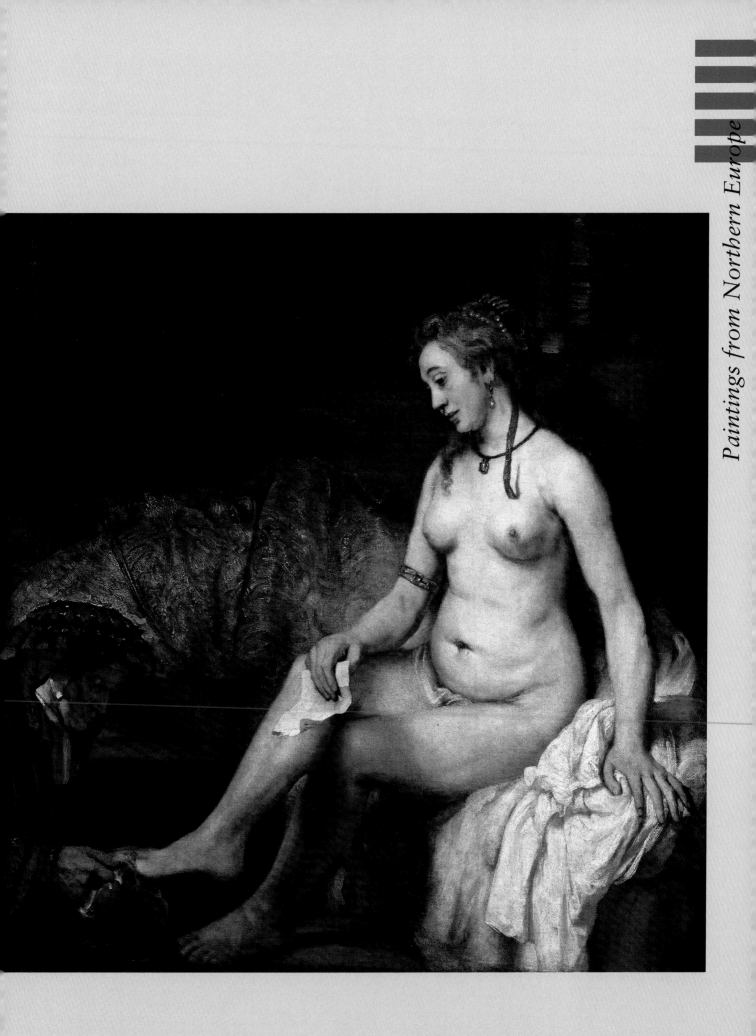

JOHANNES VERMEER (1632–1675)

The Lacemaker

Circa 1669–70. Oil on canvas glued on wood, 24 x 21 cm.

Rediscovered at the end of the nineteenth century, Vermeer is known only from
some two-score paintings. This is the smallest of them, and one of the most
beautiful. In common with other Dutch painters of the seventeenth century,
Vermeer liked to depict scenes of domestic life with a realism that sometimes
hides a moralising message. But he stands out for the extraordinary formal
rigour of his painting. In its extreme concision, *The Lacemaker* presents a
synthesis of his pictorial experiments. The tight framing concentrates attention
on the main motif, whose light colours stand out against the dark table and
cushion. Vermeer plays on optical effects, contrasting the blurring of the
foreground with the clarity of the hands and the threads they are pulling.
He varies his texture, from rough (wherever the surface of the canvas is
manifest) to smooth (the forehead and hair). The peacefully diffused light
helps transform this scene of everyday life into a miracle of painting.

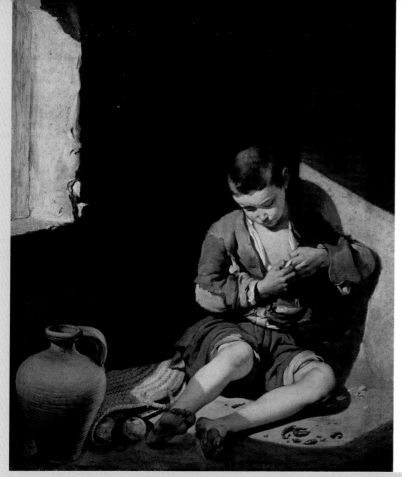

◀ Bartolomé Esteban Murillo (1618–1682)
The Young Beggar
Circa 1645–50. Oil on canvas, 134 x 110 cm.

This famous canvas is representative
of the realist tendency in the Spanish
painting of the Golden Century. Following
the example of Caravaggio, Murillo, like
Velázquez and Ribera, sought to represent
various aspects of popular life. Here,
a young boy delouses himself while
warming himself in the square of sunlight
from the window above.

◀ Domenikos Theotokopoulos,
known as El Greco (1541–1614)
**Christ on the Cross
Adored by Donors**
1576–79. Oil on canvas, 260 x 171 cm.

From 1838 to 1848, the Louvre was home
to the 'Spanish Museum', hundreds of
masterworks by the greatest Spanish artists
collected by King Louis-Philippe. That
superb ensemble was broken up in 1853
and, sadly, this was the only painting
the Louvre managed to recover.
In this magnificent example of El Greco's
art, with its elongated, flame-like twisted
figure and jagged sky, the whole cosmos
seems to be going into fusion as a result
of the artist's visionary fever.

▶ Francisco de Goya y Lucientes
(1746–1828)
**The Countess del Carpio,
Marques de La Solana**
1794–95. Oil on canvas, 181 x 122 cm.

Here, Goya displays his full genius as
a portraitist. The pared-down composition,
the dazzling handling and the refined
palette go hand in hand with psychological
penetration and insight. This young
aristocrat seems to be the prisoner
of a solitude and fragility that make
her extremely moving, and that her fate
would confirm: 'La Solana' died young,
shortly after Goya painted this portrait.

▲ THOMAS GAINSBOROUGH (1727–1788)
CONVERSATION IN A PARK
1745. Oil on canvas, 73 x 68 cm.

Gainsborough was both a marvellous
portraitist and one of the first great
landscape painters of the English School.
Here he tries his hand at the typically
English genre of the 'conversation piece',
in which the social portrait takes on the
informal, familiar tone of the genre scene.
It is thought that in this painting
he represented himself with his young
wife, in the year of their wedding.

▶ JOSEPH MALLORD WILLIAM TURNER
(1775–1851)
**LANDSCAPE WITH DISTANT RIVER
AND BAY**
Circa 1835–40. Oil on canvas, 94 x 124 cm.

In England, as in Germany – Protestant
countries, both – Romantic aspirations
were expressed mainly through landscape
painting. Turner was one of the boldest
artists of the first half of the nineteenth
century. If in his early days he was
influenced by the classical landscapes
of Claude Lorrain, he went on to make
increasing use of the suggestive and
dramatic power of colour. In his final
series, as here, everything dissolves
in light and verges on abstraction.

▶ SIR JOSHUA REYNOLDS (1723–1792)
MASTER HARE
1788. Oil on canvas, 77 x 63 cm.

Throughout his long career, Reynolds was a dominant figure in the English art world. This portrait of a very young child reflects the Enlightenment interest in the world of childhood and the expression of sensibility. It also exhibits the sterling qualities of an artist schooled in the examples of Flemish and Venetian art.

Visitor information

MUSÉE DU LOUVRE
75058 Paris Cedex 01, France
Tel.: (33) 01 40 20 50 50
Fax: (33) 01 40 20 54 52

Information
Every day, except Tuesday, from 9 a.m. to 6:45 p.m. (9:45 p.m. Wednesday and Friday): (33) 01 40 20 53 17.
www.louvre.fr

Access
• Galerie du Carrousel, Porte de la Pyramide or Porte des Lions (from 9 a.m. to 17:30 p.m. except Tuesday and Friday), for visitors without advance tickets or special passes.
• There is special wait-free access at Passage Richelieu, Galerie du Carrousel and Porte des Lions for holders of the following cards: Amis du Louvre, Louvre Jeunes, Musée et Monuments, Louvre Enseignant, Louvre Professionnels, art student passes, American Friends of the Louvre, special partnerships.
• Disabled visitors with mobility impairments have direct priority access at the Pyramid entrance.
Free wheelchairs are available.
(Info.: handicap@louvre.fr

Transport
• Métro: Palais-Royal/Musée du Louvre station, lines 1 and 7.
• Bus: nos. 21, 24, 27, 39, 48, 68, 69, 72, 81, 95.

• The Paris Open Tour bus stops in front of the Pyramid.
• An underground car park is accessible by Avenue du Général Lemonier. Open daily from 7 a.m. to 23 p.m.
• Batobus: get off at the Louvre stop, Quai François Mitterrand.

Opening times
• The museum is open from 9 a.m. to 6 p.m. except on Tuesday and the following holidays: 1 January, 1 May, 11 November and 25 December. The permanent collection and temporary exhibitions will close at 5 p.m. on 24 and 31 December, 2008 (Wednesday).
• The museum is open until 10 p.m. on Wednesday and Friday evenings (access via the Pyramid and Galerie du Carrousel).
• The museum does not have enough staff to keep the entire museum open every day. A yearly calendar lists which rooms are open and closed for each day of the week.
Information: 33 (0)1 40 20 53 17
www.louvre.fr ('Visit' heading, then 'Practical Information' and 'Opening Hours').

Free admission
Access to the museum is free on the first Sunday of each month, all day long, for all visitors.

Online tickets
Tickets purchased online can be used on any day when the museum is open. Ticketweb, FNAC, TicketNet.

Aids and amenities
The Louvre has a wide range of aids and amenities from floor plans, audio guides, and program listings to cafés, media centres, and a bookstore.
• Audioguides are available in English, French, Spanish, German, Italian, Japanese and Korean.
• CyberLouvre allows visitors to get to know the collections and history of the Louvre by consulting CDs and DVDs. These are openly available every day except Tuesday from 9 a.m. to 5:45 p.m.
Access: Allée du Grand Louvre (passage linking the Hall Napoléon to the Galerie du Carrousel).
• Multimedia Room, Near Eastern Antiquities.
Three interactive terminals provide access to an encyclopaedia of Near Eastern and Islamic art and civilisation. With maps.
Department of Near Eastern Antiquities, Richelieu wing, Hall Colbert, Salle 1 bis. The centre is open to the general public during museum opening hours.
• Department of Decorative Arts multimedia centre: information (books, photographs) on the collection. Richelieu wing, 1st floor, Salle 94.

Open Monday to Friday 10 a.m.
to 12:30 p.m. and 2 p.m. to 5:30 p.m..
Closed Tuesday. Free access,
except to the computer database.
• Department of Prints and Drawings
multimedia centre.
Flore wing, Porte des Lions.
Free access from Monday to Friday
from 1 p.m. to 6 p.m.

Photographs
Works in the permanent collections
may be photographed or filmed for
visitors' private use.
Please note that flashes and other
lighting devices are strictly prohibited.

Groups
• Group tours (maximum: 25 persons)
with an official guide.
Guided tours given by official guides
of the Musées Nationaux are available
in French, English, German, Spanish,
Italian, Portuguese, and Russian, as
well as in French sign language (LSF).
Each tour lasts ninety minutes.
Reservation by downloaded form,
by phone (33 (0)1 40 20 51 77) or
by fax (33 (0)1 40 20 84 58).
• Groups with their own guides
Advance reservations are required for
groups of seven persons (including
your own guide or group leader) and
more.

Auditorium
Located under the Pyramid,
the Auditorium proposes seasonal
programmes of talks, concert and films
related to the collections and events
at the museum.

Free services
Coat and luggage checks, first aid
room. Loan of walking sticks, strollers,
and wheelchairs.

Restaurant and cafés
A restaurant ('Le Grand Louvre',
33 (0)1 40 20 53 41), a cafeteria and
five cafés are located around the
museum spaces. They are open on
museum opening days and cater for
both individual visitors and groups.

Bookstore
The bookstore (in Hall Napoléon
under the Pyramid) is open every day
from 9:30 a.m. to 7 p.m. (and until
9:45 p.m. on Wednesdays and
Fridays).
The Chalcographie (prints and
engravings) store sells prints made by
the Réunion des Musées Nationaux
from the museum's collection of
original copper plates – in all, more
than 16,000 prints and engravings.

Annual Passes
• Carte Louvre Jeunes.
For visitors aged under 26.
adhesion.louvrejeunes@louvre.fr
• Carte Louvre Enseignants (teachers)
louvreenseignants@louvre.fr

• Carte Louvre Professionnels
louvreprofessionnels@louvre.fr

La Société des Amis du Louvre
The Société des Amis du Louvre
("Friends of the Louvre") was set up
to support the development of the
museum's collections. It can be joined
at the desk in Galerie du Carrousel,
Allée du Grand Louvre, or on the
website (www.amis-du-louvre.org).
Membership brings numerous
advantages, including free admission
to the permanent collections and
temporary exhibitions, with priority
access through Passage Richelieu.

Prints and Drawings
Housed in the Flore wing, the
Department of Prints and Drawings
(one of the Louvre's eight departments)
conserves some 140,000 works on
paper in every technique. Because of
their sensitivity to light, these works
are shown only in temporary
exhibitions or by appointment, in the
Cabinet des Arts Graphiques.

The Pavillon des Sessions
Since 2000 the former Pavillon des
Sessions has presented 120
masterpieces from Africa, Asia,
Oceania and the Americas.
This selection constitutes an extension
of the Musée du Quai Branly.
Entrance via the Porte des Lions.

2nd Floor

- ◼ French Paintings
- ▨ German, Flemish and Dutch Paintings
- ◼ Prints and Drawings

1st Floor

- ◼ Decorative Arts
- ◻ Egyptian Antiquities
- ◼ Greek, Etruscan and Roman Antiquities
- ◼ Paintings
- ◻ Prints and Drawings

Ground Floor

- ◼ Sculptures
- ◻ Oriental Antiquities
- ◼ Egyptian Antiquities
- ◼ Greek, Etruscan and Roman Antiquities
- ◼ Arts of Africa, Asia, Oceania and the Americas

Lower Ground Floor

- ◼ Arts of Islam
- ◼ Sculptures
- ◻ Egyptian Antiquities
- ◼ Greek, Etruscan and Roman Antiquities
- ◼ History of the Louvre The Medieval Louvre

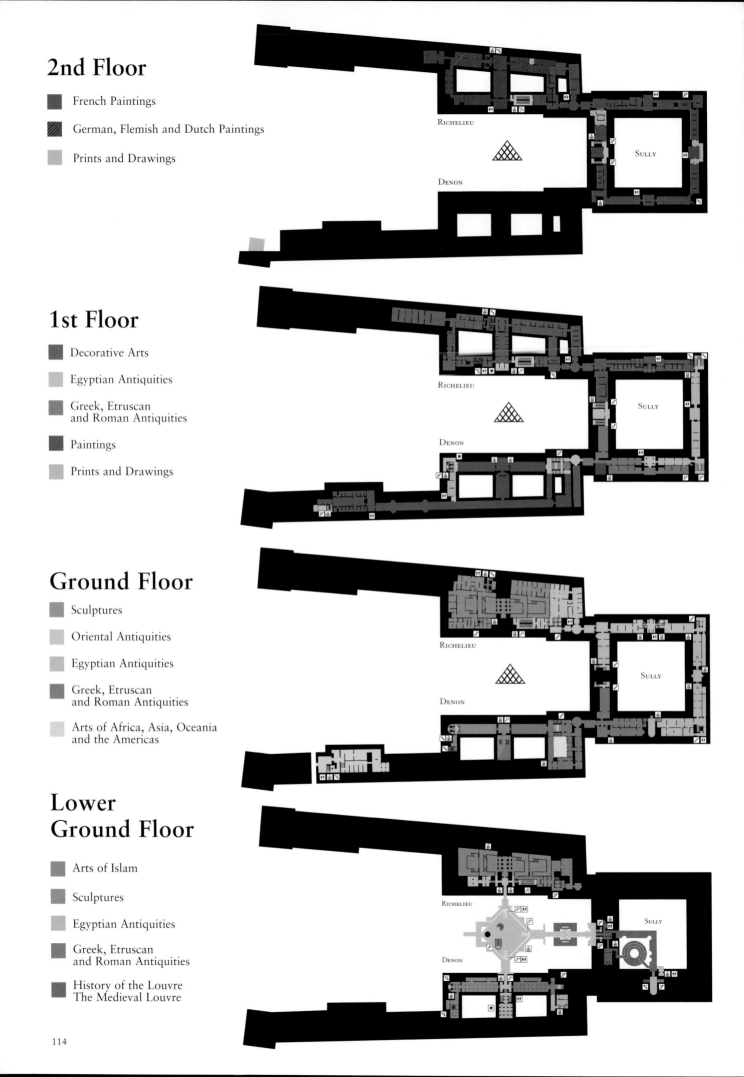

RICHELIEU

SULLY

DENON

Special issues of Connaissance des Arts
Publisher: Nicolas Beytout – Editor-in-chief: Guy Boyer @ Director of Development: Philippe Thomas @ – Editor: Pascale Bertrand @ – Picture Editor: Diane de Contades @ – Secretariat-Interpreter: Kathryn Levesque @ Production Manager: Sandrine Lebreton @ – Sales assistant: Hortense de Marchéville @
The people whose names are followed by the symbol @ have an e-mail address, to be composed as follows: firstnameinitialsurname@cdesarts.com
Production of this issue: Layout: Isabelle de Vassart-Roller – Copy editor: Chantal Charpentier – Translation: Charles Penwarden.
Photographic credits: ©RMN/G. Blot: cover, pp. 16-17h, 37, 78, 79, 83h, 84h, 103b, 106, 107, 108; ©RMN/H. Lewandowski: cover, pp. 4bg, 5h, 10b, 24d, 25d, 26b, 28, 30b, 34, 40, 41, 42, 44, 45, 46b, 47, 48, 50, 51h, 56g, 76, 77, 87h, 89, 90, 92, 94hd, 95, 104h, 111; ©RMN/H. Lewandowski/Th. Le Mage: cover, pp. 5bm, 72, 96, 97; ©RMN/F. Raux: cover, pp. 32, 33, 80h, 98b; ©H. Champollion/Akg-images: cover, lower; © Lois Lammerhuber/Photoagentur Lammerhuber: endpaper, front, pp. 4hg, 7, endpaper, back; ©RMN/G. Blot/H.Lewandowski: pp. 2-3, 43; ©RMN/C. Rose: pp.4hm, 8-9, 10h, 20-21; ©RMN/Droits réservés: pp. 4hd, 14, 22, 26h, 27, 51b, 57, 68h, 71h, 100-101, 110; ©RMN/Ch. Jean: pp. 4bd, 54, 58b, 62, 102, 109h; ©RMN/M. Beck-Coppola: pp. 5bg, 12-13, 64, 67, 70; ©Eyedea/Van Der Hilst Robert: pp. 5bd,112-113; ©RMN/G.Blot /Ch. Jean: pp. 11, 59g; ©Bridgeman Art Library: pp. 15, 18-19; ©RMN/Ch. Jean/J. Schormans: pp. 24g; ©RMN/D. Arnaudet/G. Blot: pp. 25g, 86, 87b; ©RMN/Les frères Chuzeville: pp. 30h, 31, 36, 69; ©RMN/R.-G. Ojéda: pp. 35, 46h, 56d, 58h, 59d, 60, 61, 63, 74, 75b, 80b, 83b, 91h, 99, 104b, 109b; ©RMN/J.-G. Berizzi: pp. 52, 66d, 71b, 82, 84b, 93, 94bg, 103h; Musée des Arts Décoratifs, Paris/photo: L. Sully Jaulmes: pp. 53; ©RMN/D. Arnaudet: pp. 66hg, 68b, 85, 88; ©RMN/R.-G. Ojéda/Th. Le Mage: pp. 75h; ©RMN/Th. Le Mage: pp. 81, 91b, 98h; ©RMN/J. Schormans: pp. 105; © graphic design: Bettina Pell: pp. 114; back cover: © RMN / G.Blot / PCF & P.
Distribution of special issues: Subscriptions: + 33 1 44 88 55 25 – Sale of individual issues: + 33 1 44 88 55 17
The special issues of Connaissance des Arts are published by SFPA © 2008 Société Française de Promotion Artistique
51, rue Vivienne, 75095 Paris Cedex 02 – Tel.: 01 44 88 55 00 – Fax: 01 44 88 51 88 – e-mail: cda@cdesarts.com
Manager: Jean-Jacques Schardner – R.C. Paris 75 B 304 951 460 – Commission: 1005 K 79964 – ISSN 1242-9198
Legal copyright: 2nd quarter 2008. H. S. 357/1. Photoengraving: Planète Couleurs. Printed by Kapp-Lahure-Jombart in Evreux.